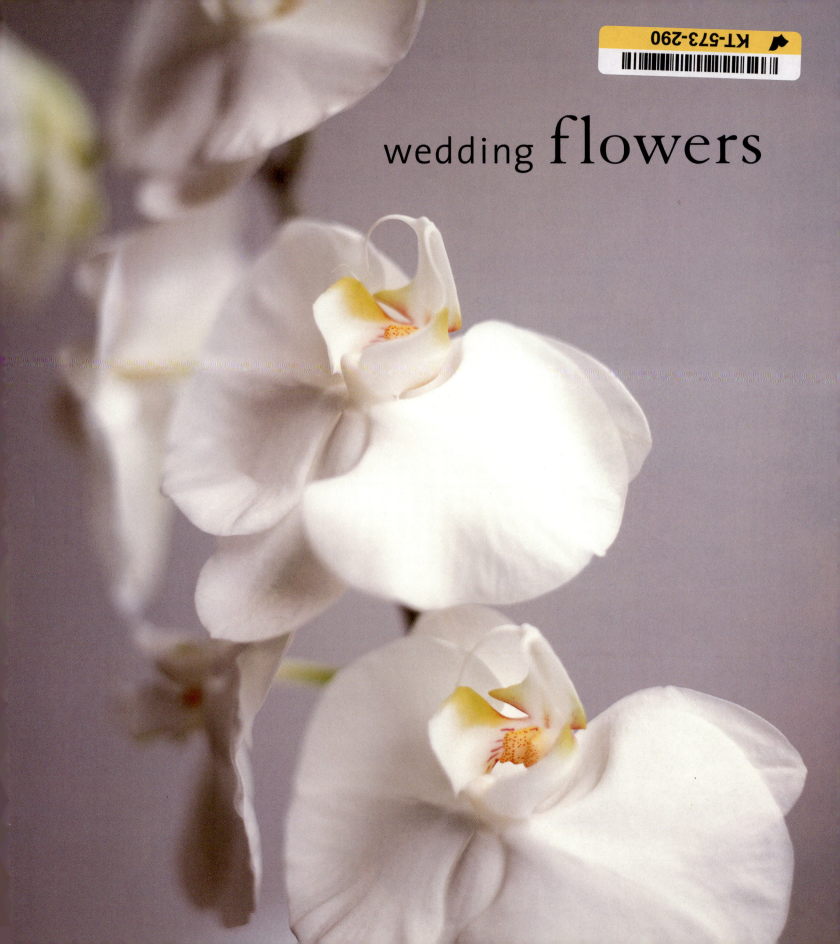

wedding flowers

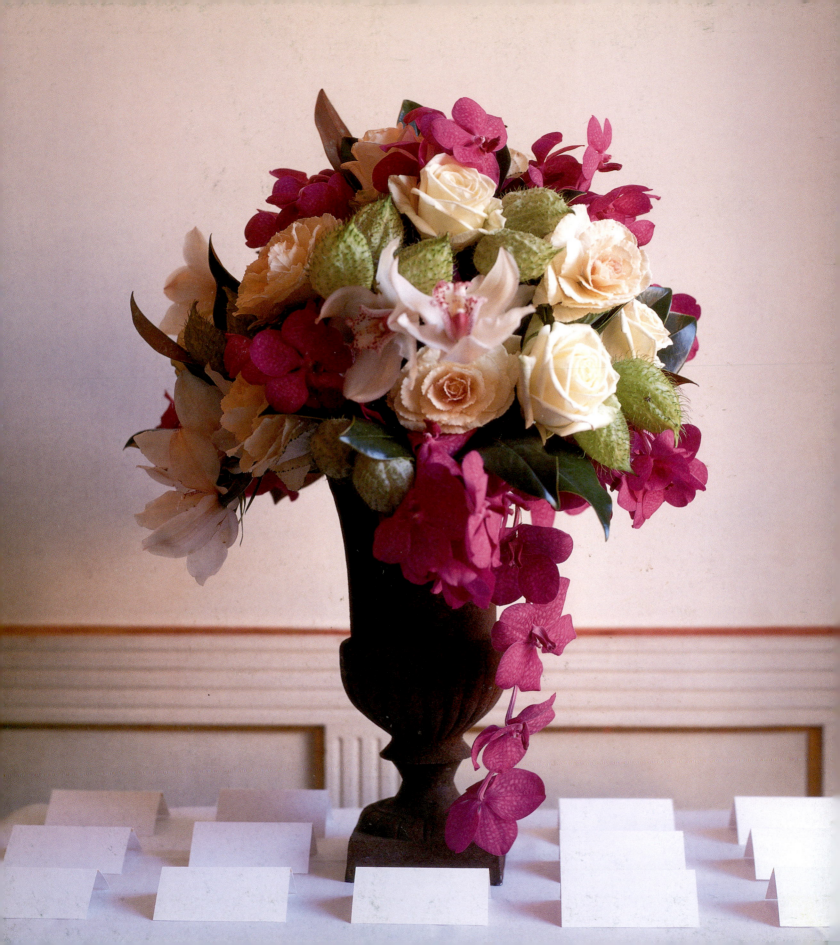

PHOTOGRAPHY BY CHRIS TUBBS

wedding flowers

paula pryke

jacqui
small

First published in 2004 by **Jacqui Small**, an imprint of Aurum Press Ltd,
7 Greenland Street, London NW1 0ND

Text copyright Paula Pryke 2004. Photography, design and layout copyright
Jacqui Small 2004.
Additional location photography by Contre-Jour

PUBLISHER Jacqui Small
ART DIRECTOR Valerie Fong
PHOTOGRAPHY Chris Tubbs
EDITORIAL MANAGER Vicki Vrint
PRODUCTION Geoff Barlow

ISBN 978 1 903221 18 1
A catalogue record for this book is available from the British Library.

10 9 8 7 6

*For all the brides and grooms, and their loved
ones, who have let me be a part of their very
special day and who gave me the honour
of designing decorations for their weddings.*

PRINTED AND BOUND IN CHINA

contents

6   choosing your flowers

16   seasonal flowers

42   bouquets

64   floral accessories

86   ceremony flowers

104   reception flowers

144   floral colour glossary

158   index

160   acknowledgements

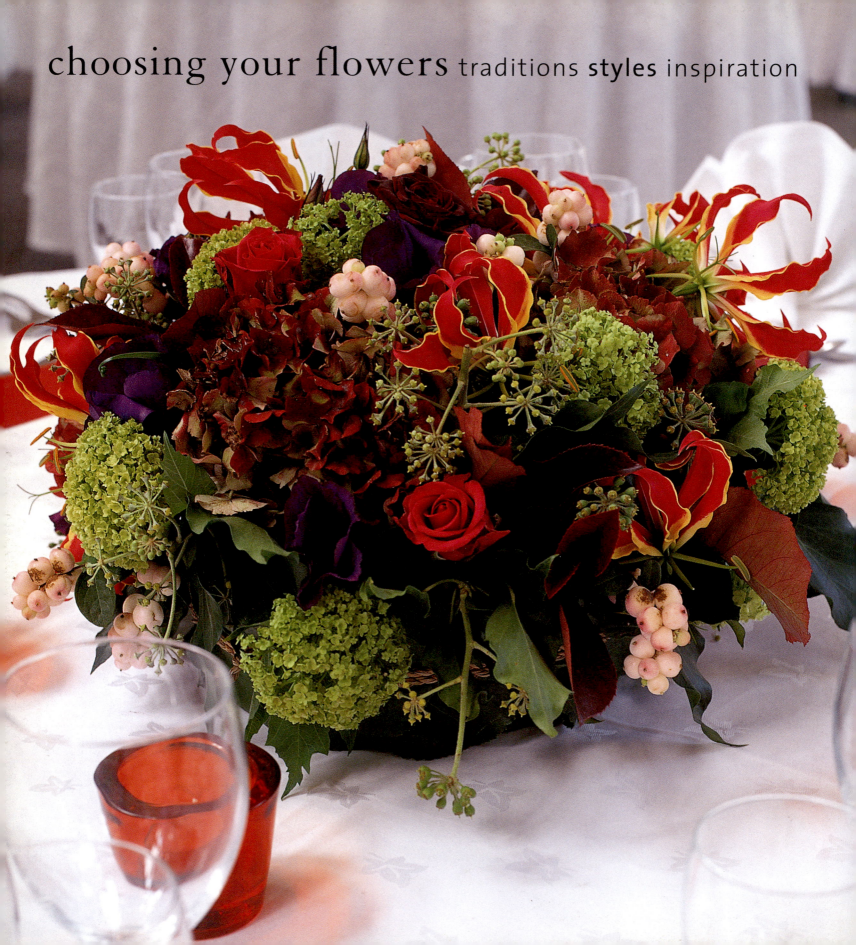

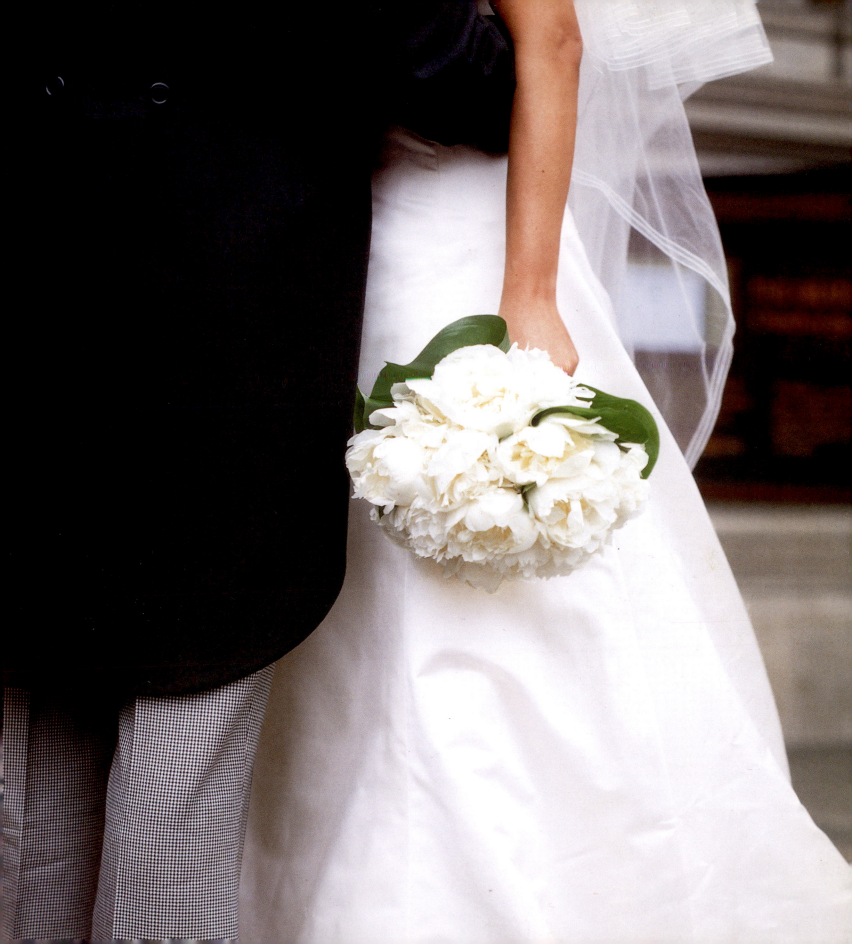

the role of flowers

Flowers and foliage have been an integral part of wedding ceremonies around the world since time began. As tokens of love exchanged between men and women they have a deep resonance in our romantic life and psyche. Flowers unite people and instantly provide links between strangers, so they are vital to the heart of any wedding celebration. We all appreciate their aesthetic beauty, their perfect form, colour or heavenly fragrance but our ancestors appreciated them more for their meanings and their uses, and these still affect our choices today.

Flowers have featured in the beliefs, art and medicine of our predecessors for thousands of years. They play a part in our myths and legends, and in religion and worship. They have become symbols of a whole range of human and spiritual experience and were originally chosen for this symbolism and their fragrance, rather than their appearance or colour. Greek brides carried marjoram to bring joy, Roman brides wove sprigs of rosemary into their headdresses to ensure devotion and love, and to make sure their marriages endured. Medieval brides wove together fresh garlands of flowers and herbs to wear on their heads, hoping that these would ward off evil spirits and bless their marriages with love, joy, good health, purity, fidelity and fertility.

Many plants and flowers were given these symbolic meanings because of their nature or habitat. The box tree, for example, was thought to mean stoicism as it is evergreen and unaffected by the seasons. Lily-of-the-valley was considered an emblem of chastity and humility because of the bowed nature of the bells and the pure white blooms. Today, brides may choose this delicate flower for its divine scent and the fabulous look of a posy of a mass of these lovely blooms.

floral traditions
The first wedding that really influenced the style of the modern ceremony was the marriage of Queen Victoria of England to Prince Albert – a great romance. Orange blossom was the flower of the day. It has a very long association with wedding nuptials. Juno, the Greek goddess of marriage, gave a wreath of orange blossom to Jupiter, her bridegroom, on their wedding night. In ancient times it signified fertility, but during the Victorian period it came to symbolize chastity and purity.

I suspect that the 'orange blossom' that Queen Victoria wore was philadelphus (commonly known as orange blossom) unless blooms were gathered from orange trees in her estate greenhouses! Both flowers are extremely beautiful, as delicate as lace and as fragrant as the most precious bottle of perfume. Neither transports very easily though, so unless you are lucky enough to be marrying in an orange grove or in a garden filled with philadelphus you may have to use vines of stephanotis or

jasmine, or the sweet flowers of gardenias to add the fragrance. Scent is one ingredient of the perfect wedding that has endured the centuries. Fragrant herbs, foliage and flowers help to create a unique floral perfume for your special day. For me the scent of 'Star Gazer' lilies and lily-of-the-valley will always bring back very happy memories of my wedding.

Queen Victoria's wedding also made the white wedding gown popular and it became common for brides to hold a tight posy featuring concentric circles of all-white flowers, still known to this day as a 'Victorian posy'. As fashions changed and floristry techniques improved, cascading 'shower' bouquets became popular. They were often very heavy as their mechanics were crude by today's standards.

Very often the bride would give a flower from her bouquet to her bridesmaids, and occasionally bouquets were made of composite posies so that each maid could take flowers away. Sprigs of herbs and flowers were often pinned into the bodice of the bridal gown or attached to the gown itself. From the turn of the century bridesmaids would also carry flowers, either huge wicker baskets filled with blooms or a floral staff. In more austere and religious circumstances a bible or prayer book was decorated with flowers and carried during the ceremony.

Historically the main influences on wedding fashion have been economic. Not surprisingly when the world is enjoying peace and prosperity lavish wedding style is in vogue. During the prosperous years of the twenties some of our more elaborate fashion traditions came into force. Wedding arches, candelabras and grand pedestals of flowers became the norm among the social elite and the role of the wedding florist emerged. Second World War and post-war brides, by contrast, had to forsake many wedding traditions and wear simple dresses often made by themselves or their family, and carry simple, wired, white posies of flowers usually fashioned into a cascade, crescent or a shower. Locally grown lilies, orchids, roses and carnations were often mixed with fronds of asparagus ferns.

OPPOSITE A modern take on the traditional bridesmaid's basket. This zinc container is filled with summer flowers including roses and sweet peas, and features garden fillers such as astrantia and *Stachys byzantina*. Baskets such as this are suitable for younger bridesmaids to carry easily. **ABOVE, CLOCKWISE FROM TOP** The bridal party awaiting the arrival of the bride, holding classic posies of white sweet peas and lime-green *Viburnum opulus*; A simple, traditional posy of lily-of-the-valley; A typical Victorian posy consisting of concentric circles of different varieties of flowers.

The Flower Power period of the sixties ironically saw little demand for extravagant flowers and the trend for formal marriages almost disappeared as intimate weddings became popular. The wedding of Lady Diana Spencer to the Prince of Wales (heir to the British throne) in 1981, however, signalled a change from informal weddings to more traditional and lavish ceremonies. Diana's dress and cascading bouquet of intricately wired flowers marked a new trend for traditional shower bouquets, almost reminiscent of the twenties. The bouquet was well over a metre long, and filled with many scented flowers. Bouquets like this are costly to produce both in terms of using the best and most exquisite blooms and also in labour, so this is an expensive option.

choosing your flowers

For better or worse, for richer or poorer, fashions and trends are continually evolving and re-emerging, and choosing wedding flowers can be one of a bride's most daunting tasks. With modern farming techniques, you can have practically any flower your heart desires at almost any time of the year and the choice of blooms is immense. There is an extraordinary repertoire of vibrant colours, intricate patterns and alluring scents to choose from.

Beautiful weddings can be affordable on any budget and the key is to be realistic about what you can achieve. Start by deciding which flowers are essential, then move on to your 'wish list'. That way you can keep your needs and your desires in perspective – and spare your bridegroom and father a shock! Often the cost of the flowers is split between both families – usually the bridegroom pays for the bridal bouquets and the decorations for the ceremony, and the bride (or her family) pays for the decorations for the wedding breakfast. With couples marrying much later in life, they often foot at least some, if not all, of the bill themselves. A sensible benchmark is to spend approximately the same on the flowers as you spend on your wedding dress.

In many cases your florist will be able to help you with a lot of the details and once you have found someone you would like to work with you can use them as a sounding board for your ideas. Often they will have arranged flowers in the same venue or similar circumstances and will be able to give you lots of suggestions – and possibly show you pictures from their portfolio – to help you choose your look.

BELOW, CLOCKWISE FROM TOP This is a natural, round bouquet using mixed colours, suitable for a country wedding. It includes lilac *Rosa* 'Blue Gene' and *Rosa* 'Blue Curiosa' mixed with the white 'Avalanche' rose and the lime-green blossom of *Viburnum opulus*; A classic summer bouquet of white peonies edged with hosta leaves. Round bouquets of a single variety suit any style of wedding gown; A contemporary and elegant over-arm bouquet of white calla lilies with green 'Midori' anthuriums. The shapes of these flowers perfectly suit this style of bouquet.

wedding styles

Broadly speaking wedding flowers can be categorized as classic, romantic or alternative in style, and the look you go for will probably be influenced by your choice of venue. Classic flowers can be contemporary or historical and are by far the most popular choice among brides as they suit the most commonly used venues, such as hotel banqueting rooms and halls. This style also suits traditional ceremony venues. Classic white or cream arrangements are perfect for the interior of a church, which may provide a grand marble backdrop. The classic style is also the most economic to create and by using the best of seasonal flowers and foliage you are almost always guaranteed an elegant and opulent look.

The romantic look encompasses various styles, using scented and seasonal flowers in a soft and rustic way. Lots of delicate flowers may be massed together or arranged loosely. This feminine feel suits almost any venue but my personal favourite for this rural feel is, of course, a country wedding. Simply woven decorations including swags, garlands and arches made from

seasonal blooms such as wheat, poppies, daisies and herbs are the essence of this style. The more decorations, the more draped ivies and candles the better.

Alternative or innovative style involves a confident and striking theme, which can be minimalist. Usually a blank canvas such as a smart restaurant or a stylish all-white marquee is the best backdrop to display this kind of strong design, rather than a traditional hotel banqueting room. It suits unusual venues and urban weddings such as museums or art galleries and is often a more common choice for a second wedding. The innovative bride may choose to use deep colours (almost-black tulips and calla lilies) in a structured architectural design or masses of one type of flower for all the decorations (pure white phalaenopsis orchids, for example). Beware of this look if you are on a budget as it seems simple to create, but these single blooms are very expensive.

setting limitations
Often brides fall into one of two categories; those who have been planning their wedding since nursery and have a very firm idea of how they want their day to be and those who have never given it much thought and perhaps do not have time to worry about the details. If you have no idea about budget you will need to use wedding books and magazines to get yourself up to speed. (These are also a useful source of contacts when gathering prices.) Regardless of the style of wedding you choose it is advisable to determine what is affordable. It is not prudent to launch into a celebration that is going to lead you and your new husband into financial anxieties before the honeymoon is over.

If you are stretching the budget there are a few things you could consider. Certain times of year are cheaper for weddings than others, most venues have a sliding scale of tariffs with June being more expensive than January, for example. Some venues are less expensive if you choose a day other than Saturday or Sunday. Look for a venue that will allow you to find your own caterer and provide your own wines and champagne. (Although you will have to pay corkage you will still get better value.)

Keep the number of attendants down. The more bridesmaids, ushers, groomsmen, flower girls and ring bearers you have the grander the wedding becomes and the more outfits and presents have to be bought. Also think seriously about who you want to invite – you may decide not to extend the invitations to your friends' children or latest 'date'!

For the decorations choose a mass of seasonal flowers and use berries and fruits in arrangements as they are much less expensive than blooms. Failing that go to a garden centre, nursery or farmers' market and buy some lovely flowering houseplants that, cleverly wrapped, will work as centrepieces. I have seen African violets, lavender and Marguerite daisies – or even chrysanthemums – work well when presented in this way.

Look out for inexpensive votives that will add ambiance to the table. (You will also be able to re-use these at future parties.) Groups of candles work well for an evening function, just edge in ivy and assorted greenery

ABOVE The choice of a strong colour for the bridal gown demands flowers that are of the same intensity as the fabric of the dress. The red 'Grand Prix' roses and Singapore orchids perfectly complement the gown, while the lime-green cymbidium orchids and the green amaranthus make a striking contrast. The trailing shower bouquet balances the full skirt of the gown beautifully.

or float one or two flower heads with some floating candles in bowls. For a winter wedding candles in mounds of shelled nuts with the odd clementine is also very effective. Another option is to use a bowl of colourful fruit, arranged well. (Your caterer should be able to hire you some footed glass bowls.) That way your guests can pick too! Another inexpensive and easy option that can be most effective is to float one or two flower heads along with floating candles in a pretty bowl on each table. Whatever you do, don't stint on hiring your photographer as he or she will provide your reminder of the special day. Take great care in choosing this trusted professional. Whatever ceremony you choose – and however you decide to decorate it – remember that all brides look fantastic on the day and every wedding has its own unique moments and beauty.

themes

One of the drawbacks with planning a wedding is that there are so many ways you can personalize your special day. Although that can be quite liberating it can also make you a slave to your wedding day, so beware! A theme can be a lovely idea but when you find yourself locked onto the Internet looking for an obscure variety of favours or peppermint-coloured ostrich feathers be easy on yourself! Always remember, throughout the planning of your wedding, that your aesthetic should be to create an original, striking and holistic theme that lends dignity, beauty and joy to even the smallest of weddings.

I have had the pleasure of arranging flowers for a range of themes – from *A Midsummer Night's Dream* and *Swan Lake* to Winnie the Pooh. Regal figures such as Princess Grace and Princess Margaret have influenced weddings, as have Hollywood movies like *Moulin Rouge* and *Gone with the Wind*. Whatever you choose, flowers can complement your theme – a pony and trap can be decked out with buckets of wild blooms or a much-loved sports car or vintage vehicle can be trimmed with flowers.

inspiration

Sometimes the inspiration for a theme can come from the most unlikely places. One bride used lilac feathers for her invitations, which started a very strong colour theme. In the end, the wedding was enhanced by lavender-scented candles, bowls of lilac sweets, masses of lilac roses (including 'Blue Curiosa' and 'Sterling Silver') and other lilac summer flowers including ageratum, sweet peas and lisianthus. Each guest was presented with a lilac box containing delicious violet creams, topped with a crystallized violet. One very beautiful – but staggeringly expensive – theme used gardenia blooms by the thousand to create one of the most fragrant weddings I have every witnessed.

Another bride used citrus fruits as a theme taking her husband's business (importing these fruits) as inspiration. The celebrations started with citrus cocktails and Bucks Fizz. The tables were decorated with small kumquats in vases topped with orange Icelandic poppies and mounds of orange ranunculus. The top table was garlanded with bunches of smilax and kumquats, and trimmed with pips of stephanotis. For the larger arrangements, topiary pyramids of citrus fruits were created with a few stephanotis pips and lime leaves. Large vases were lined with large cut-orange slices and filled with long-stemmed, orange 'French' tulips. The hors d'oeuvres included a salad with pink grapefruit and of course the cake was trimmed with kumquats and candied oranges. Each guest's place was marked with a jar of home-made marmalade for them to take home.

For my own wedding I used the theme of harvest, which appealed to me as I was brought up in arable farming

country. Wheat featured on the invitations, the name cards and, of course, in the decorations. Although it's not my favourite flower, it set the perfect tone for my late summer wedding. Sunflowers are also a popular choice for late summer weddings and, at one I attended, the place names were printed on packets of sunflower seeds for the guests to take away and plant as a memento the following year.

Wines and vines are a popular theme with many marriages taking place in vineyards or with a love of wine acting as inspiration for a theme for the tables. For one vineyard wedding I attended, candelabras were covered in old vines and then swathed with young green grapes and clusters of 'Black Baccara' roses, the colour of a perfect claret wine.

Another bride chose a favourite Henry David Thoreau quote, 'Go confidently in the direction of your dreams', and had a calligrapher write it round the middle of the dining tables in lavender ink. She filled the centre of the table with lavender and sweet-pea arrangements encircled by masses of nightlights (30 per table) to beautiful effect.

Countries can also provide inspiration whether it's a favourite holiday spot, or the location of the proposal. The Provençal region of France with its olive trees, geraniums, sunflowers and lavender works well, as does Spanish style, with masses of oleander, bougainvilleas and a really bright theme. Moroccan style is another very popular choice and we have themed many weddings around the feel of the balmy climate of North Africa and its tradition for decorating with bright colours.

wedding traditions
Whatever your theme and choice of flowers you will

ABOVE, CLOCKWISE FROM TOP When planning arrangements for the venue, two large arrangements have more impact than several smaller ones. The bronze sculpture is perfect for decorating with flowers as it is above eye-level. A carpet of rose petals, and rose chairbacks make a fragrant aisle for the bride and groom; The bride chose to carry her favourite flowers (purple sweet peas) and the colour was picked up in the larger arrangements, as well as on the tables; Massed flowerheads and candles in a perspex container create a patchwork of flowers that is simple (if expensive) to recreate.

probably want to include the time-honoured tradition of old, new, borrowed and blue. The 'old' symbolizes your previous life and ties with your family (a piece of jewellery is often used for this). Something new symbolizes the journey into your new life and this is always easy to achieve. A new perfume for your wedding will always remind you of the day. Traditionally borrowing something from a happily married couple will bring you the same good fortune. Brides often borrow their veil or a lace handkerchief or garter. And finally blue has long been associated with devotion and loyalty and is thought to ward off evil spirits. Often a little blue bow is sewn into the bridal gown or occasionally blue flowers are entwined into the bridal bouquet.

working with a florist

Like most things in life, the best way to find a florist is by personal recommendation, but wedding magazines can also be a useful source. Make an appointment to visit your florist so that you have time to sit down and look through their portfolio. A face-to-face meeting is important as it gives the designer a chance to get a full image of you and your personality as well as your stature and plans for the day. Professional designers are capable of working in many different styles and it is their role to create a sense of your own personal preference in your floral design. The designer should not dictate a style, but should work with you to create it.

If you are uncertain about what you want, your florist should help you develop a plan you are happy with. This will take place over a series of meetings – very rarely is everything decided on the first day –

BELOW, CLOCKWISE FROM TOP An iron arch over a gate provides the perfect floral welcome for the wedding party when decorated with flowers, including trailing phalaenopsis orchids, bowers of white bougainvillea and fronds of amaranthus. A preliminary visit with your florist will enable you to make the most of existing features at the venue, such as this archway; Garden roses and alchemilla in a round glass vase suit this chic city wedding with a white-and-green theme; This three-tiered American stacked wedding cake has been decorated simply with delicate, scented pips of tuberose.

so do not worry if you have not achieved a grand plan at your first meeting. Do give the designer your budget and ask her whether it is realistic. A real professional can help you focus on the important elements rather than anything impractical you may have on your list.

It is useful for the florist if you make your first appointment once you have chosen your venues and dress. Without this information you may find it difficult to discuss any of the details. Many brides take along images of the kind of flowers they like or even the style of arrangement they are looking for. It is also helpful to take information on your bridesmaids and flower girls including dress colour and a swatch of fabric, as well as information on the ceremony and a floorplan of the reception.

Your florist should be able to outline a costing for you and, once confirmed, it is a good idea to meet them at the venue (or the site), to go through all the details. You can also discuss table linen, napkins, candles and any other aspects of the day. Check that your final quote includes everything you requested and that the delivery addresses and times will suit your schedule.

If you employ a professional it is up to them to make sure that all your flowers are delivered and presented to you in their best condition. Bear in mind that for an opulent look your florist will be aiming to get your flowers into full bloom and will not be presenting them to you in the freshest and most closed form that you might choose if you were purchasing flowers for your home.

planning ahead
It takes at least six months to plan a formal wedding on a large scale but it is easy to arrange a less formal celebration in three months or less. Also, if you pick a popular time of the year, you will find that many venues and services get booked up ahead of time and you may have to be flexible about your date. When it comes to the flowers, you can have most varieties at most times of the year but unless you are the daughter of a millionaire (or are marrying one!) do not plan to have lily-of-the-valley on every table outside the month of May. If sweet peas are your chosen flower, it obviously makes sense to hold your wedding during the summer months rather than the depths of winter.

Generally speaking, although I am happy to source flowers out of season for any of my brides in my experience seasonal flowers tend to look more effective. Nature is a great mentor and following the trends of the season will give the most harmonious and beautiful results. The other major consideration is that certain dates are peak times for the flower industry. If you are a real romantic and decide to get married on Valentine's Day it may be difficult to get a florist to commit to arranging your wedding flowers and you will certainly spend more on them.

arranging your own flowers
If you decide to arrange some of your own flowers it is advisable to have a professional take care of your bridal bouquet and all the large assemblies or intricate, complicated designs. You will then have peace of mind that your own bouquet will look great, the flowers for the photographs will be beautiful and any large arrangements will be safely constructed.

It is important to be realistic about what you can achieve. Even if you are planning a small and intimate wedding enlist the help of some friends or family and have a clear plan of action. Make a list of all the arrangements you wish to create and the components for each one, including sundries such as floral foam and tape. It is helpful to have someone to help you lift and carry. Whatever you plan, work out a schedule that includes conditioning the flowers. They will need a long drink of tepid water to revive them (as they may have been in transit for a while) and the stems should be cut diagonally with secateurs, scissors or a knife to take up the water. It is a good idea to use flower food mixed in with the water as this improves their condition. It is also imperative to clean all your buckets first (I often use bleach for this) so that bacteria doesn't contaminate the water. Top all the buckets up and leave for at least five hours or overnight so that everything is fresh and strong when you begin to arrange your flowers.

When you have completed the arrangements top up with water mixed with flower food. You can also spray water with a misting bottle – this will enhance the life of the flowers but don't overdo it or use this method with orchids, which can mark.

The best weddings I have seen have one special formula: the bride and groom are hopelessly in love and in tune with the celebrations planned and are sharing their love with their family and friends. It is important to plan your day carefully, of

ABOVE A marquee is a blank canvas that is perfectly suited to decoration with bright coloured flowers. Tall taper candles and candelabras make the most of the space and create canopies of colour above the heads of the diners. Chairs, seat pads and linen can be hired to complement your chosen theme and will create a smart co-ordinated look.

course, but do not allow yourself to become obsessed with the details as this only leads to stress. On the day, just enjoy yourself – it will seem like the fastest day you have ever lived and will almost be over before it has started, so savour every wonderful minute of it.

Whichever floral decorations you choose and however you achieve your wedding design, your flowers will be central to the event and will symbolize the hope, love and joy of your wedding celebrations.

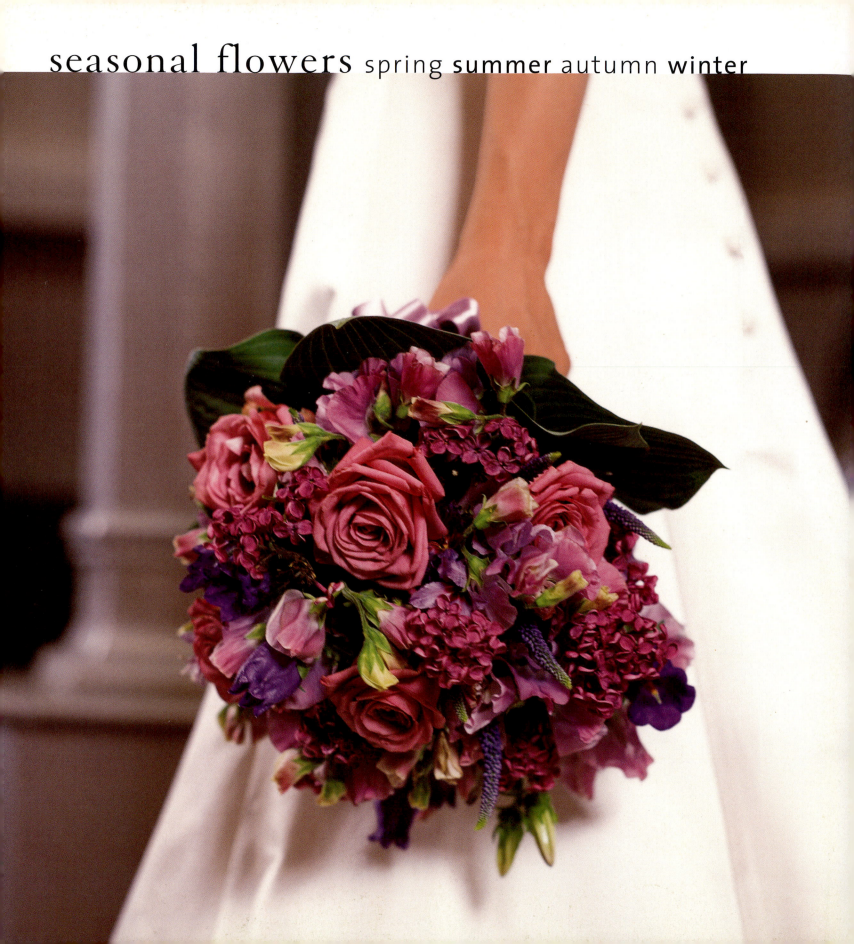

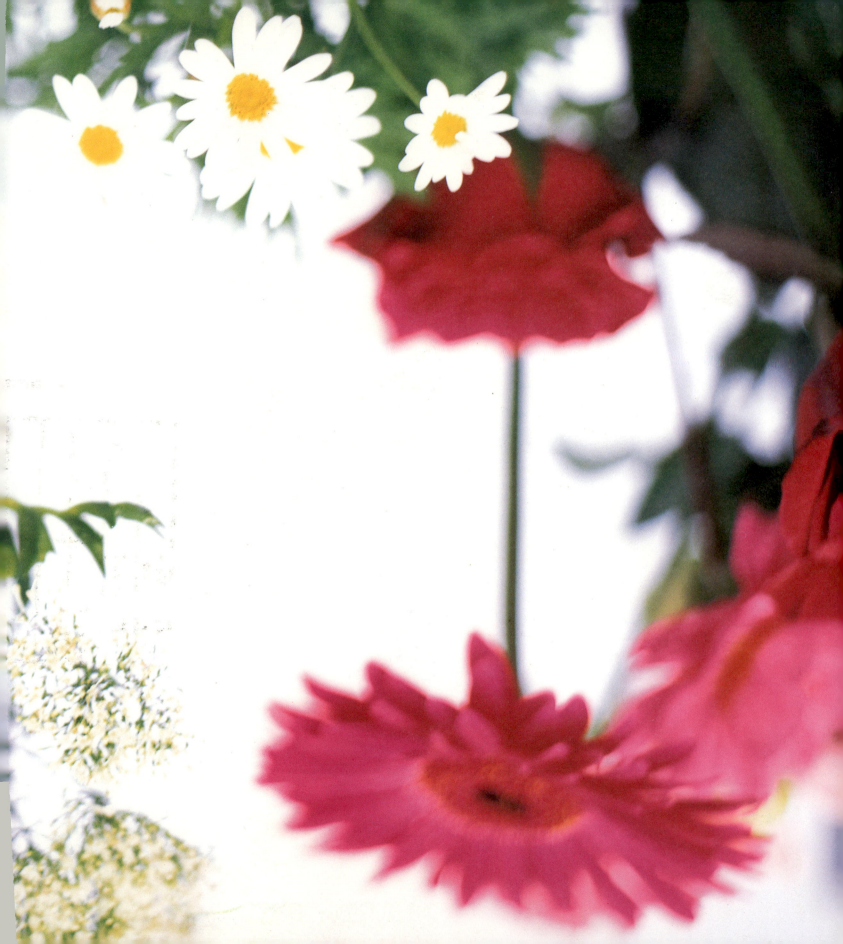

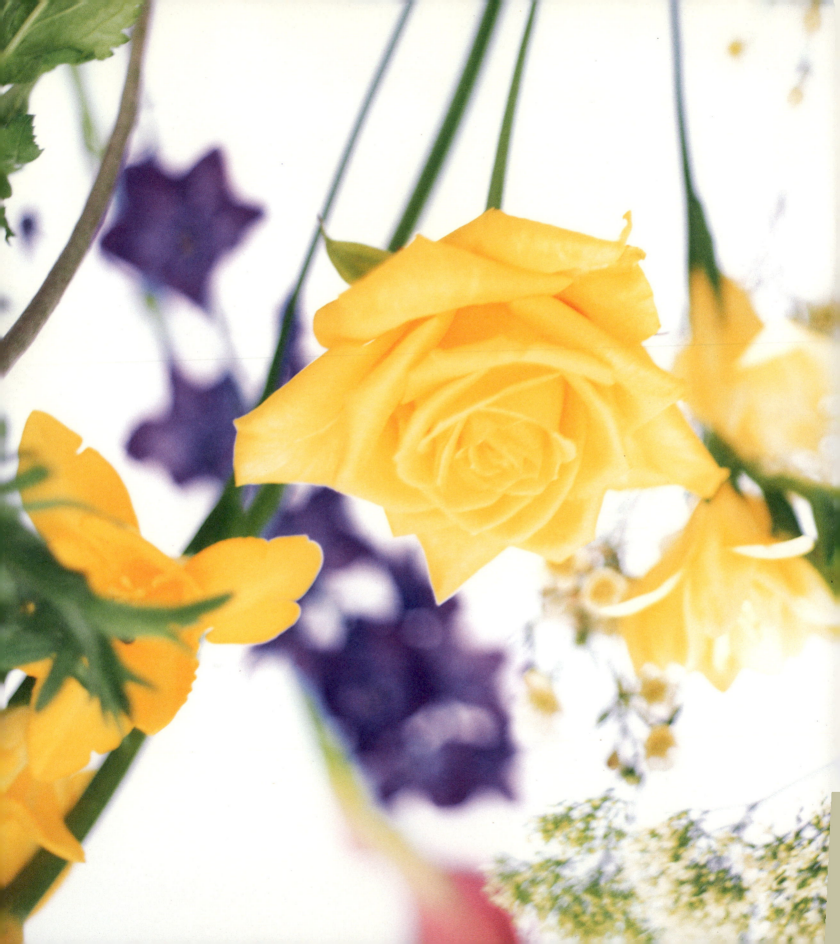

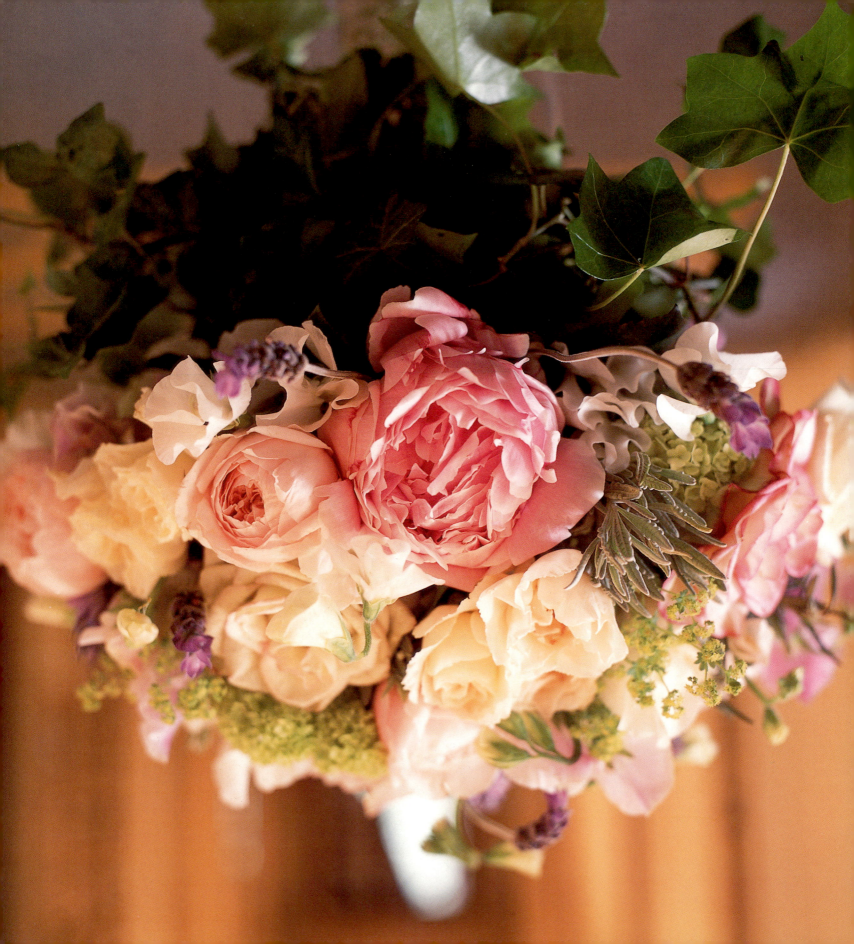

working with nature

Whatever date you choose for your wedding, seasonal flowers are by far the best option. What is the point of purchasing expensive, imported blossoms in autumn when gardens are full of jewel-like petals and flame-coloured foliage is in abundance, or in spring when nature rejoices in whites and soft colours? Our natural desires are very in tune with the seasons, so look around you for inspiration. Go for a long country walk, see what is available at your local farmers' market and go to specialist flower shops to look for the seasonal blooms.

Once I imported peonies from Australia for a November wedding in England. The long journey from the other side of the world and the lack of other seasonal flowers to accompany the blooms detracted from the natural, indescribable beauty of peonies used in season. This is partly because our perception and enjoyment of certain types of flowers (and foods) is influenced by the seasons. In spring we enjoy the pastel blooms of the early part of the year while summer brings masses of colour. As the nights draw in and the temperature drops we yearn for the warm reds and oranges of autumn, and in winter we look to whites, mossy green branches and deep red berries.

spring In spring a mass of seasonal colour is available thanks to the hybridization of one particular flower – the tulip. You can buy commercially grown tulips in over 500 varieties from pure white to marbled red-and-yellow, and the deepest black. They are an extremely versatile flower and can be made to look wild and rustic, romantic and pretty or stylized and modern, and so they suit any interior. The taller and more elegant varieties are known as 'French' tulips. My favourite spring flowers, however, are ranunculus. They are so beautiful, and are available in many colours from greeny-white to dark burgundy and even chocolate brown. Ranunculus also come in very deep and brightly coloured varieties. They make fantastic flowers for bouquets and work very well in arrangements and in wired work.

For scent in spring there are many possibilities from fragrant jasmine vines to heady hyacinths. 'Paper White' narcissi, freesias and mimosa are also very fragrant and some early blossom branches have a light scent too. Huge glass vases of pink cherry blossom look great arranged en masse. If you fancy a vibrant yellow theme with daffodils and tulips, you can add scent by using vases of the spherical blossoms of mimosa. For larger displays tall branches of forsythia work well, and yellow lilies can be found in spring and throughout the year. For deep colour anemones could be your spring choice. These elegant flowers are available in deep purple and lavender as well as bright red and deep pink. They suit both bouquets and table centres, and can be very eye-catching arranged simply, en masse. Anemones also look great bunched beneath the head to create a living tree topiary.

Other special spring flowers include muscari in blue and white, hellebores in a range of colours and the very charming snake's-head fritillary. These delicate flowers make fabulous posies and charming romantic arrangements for tables. Violets

are also at their best in the spring and although very delicate and short-lived are often associated with Valentine's Day and true love. Parma violets from Italy and English violets always come wrapped in leaves and bound with raffia to keep the stems as straight as possible and so look just perfect massed together with these leaves edging them. Early pussy-willow branches and the sweetly scented blossom of the winter-flowering viburnums are ideal for brightening up flower arrangements and posies from the beginning of the year until March.

early summer
In late spring and early summer, the most popular time of year for weddings, there is an abundance of floral material on offer. I am very drawn to the pale pinks and blues of this time of the year. I love blowsy peonies and scented garden roses for round bouquets mixed with lily-of-the-valley or aromatic lavender. Trails of honeysuckle and spray roses are just divine for longer, wilder natural bouquets. Choose stately foxgloves, sweet-scented stocks and huge hybrid delphiniums spiked with star-shaped musky lilies for large arrangements, with long branches of foliage.

If these flowers are all too blowsy and you prefer a pared-down summer theme pick a single flower for your inspiration such as the humble daisy or cornflower. I have seen many weddings using these two blooms and I have to say that the simplicity of

a bunch of daisies in a posy or in simple jugs on the table is quite breathtaking. Cornflowers also work well. They can be arranged en masse, floating in a bowl or in a simple bunch with grasses and Marguerite daisies and a few summer thistles such as eryngium or echinops.

Lavender is a favourite scented summer flower. It has inspired many of my designs. It looks good in bouquets, tied onto baskets for bridesmaids to carry or encircling arrangements. If you grow lavender then a few stems tied onto each napkin are a great way of spreading its wonderful scent and make a lovely keepsake for your guests.

The new leaf growth of large deciduous trees (including sorbus and beech) is very lush at this time of year. Great summer ground foliage includes hosta leaves and the arched stems of Solomon's seal, whose bright green hues set off mixed, rich-coloured table centres beautifully.

OPPOSITE If you have set your heart on scented garden roses, the best months to marry are between June and September when they are at their best and most plentiful. **ABOVE, CLOCKWISE FROM TOP LEFT** Here, 'Bianca Candy' roses and eustoma have been made to look more summery using 'Pink Pearl' snowberries; An alternative to wearing a corsage is to pin floral decorations onto your accessories. For this winter wedding, slipper orchids have been chosen to complement a green bag; Summer is the best time to plan your wedding if you want to use lilacs and blue flowers as there is such a wide range of blossoms to choose from, including sweet peas, hydrangeas and scabious.

late summer

The late summer months bring a wealth of striking, bright-coloured flowers such as dahlias, achilleas, sunflowers and zinnias. These suit simple displays or topiary arrangements, where their large heads make a patchwork of colour. Fabulous seed heads include the puffy, pointed pods of physalis and the seed heads of poppies and scabious. The plump berries from viburnum and spiky blackberries from the hedgerow make for mouth-watering sumptuous arrangements.

Spongy celosia is another gorgeous flower available in an array of vibrant colours. Lilies can be found all year but it is in summer that you get some of the more traditional varieties (such as 'Regalia') and the best scents. One lovely modern hybrid is 'Barbaresco', which is a deep pink colour and has the most delicious fragrance when fully opened. Old-fashioned antirrhinums are also abundant and can be found in any colour to suit your theme from bright pink to acid yellow. Cosmos also flower late and are perfect if you like a wild or understated look. Chocolate-scented brown varieties are available during August and September. Pink and white cosmos can be found in late summer.

Hydrangeas are strong now too. You can cut the florets up and include them in your headdresses. Whole flower heads look fabulous in large decorations or en masse.

autumn

Autumn brings rich colour schemes as foliage begins to display fabulous fall colours. Gladioli and chrysanthemums are in season and the slender-stemmed nerines (from perfect white and pink through to bright red) are the new jewels of the season. Massed together they make stunning round posies or great living topiary trees. Mix the blood red ones with purple callicarpa berries, brown hypericum berries and seasonal foliage and add just one or two branches of crab apples for a sumptuous autumnal arrangement. The trailing stems of love-lies-bleeding are also fabulous at this time and, used with hydrangeas and autumn foliage, can make easy work of creating large arches or decorating chuppahs.

There are also still some great lime greens including the elegant twisted spires of 'bells of Ireland'. The spider chrysanthemum 'Shamrock' is great for large displays while the smaller santini chrysanthemum 'Kermit' is great for table centres and small groupings. The green zinnia 'Envy', the lime-green-berried *Hypericum* 'Jade Flair' and the final stems of *Alchemilla mollis* add a bright tinge of green that makes any colour look fresher and more vibrant. For a blue theme in autumn use hydrangeas, delphiniums or thistles. For lilac you may get some alliums and the lilac roses 'Blue Curiosa' and 'Sterling Silver', while gladioli, lisianthus and trachelium are all available in a range of lilac and purple hues.

For me, though, an autumn wedding is the best opportunity to make use of the fruit that is abundant and inexpensive at this time of year. It is an excellent time to take a harvest theme and use wheat, barley, hops, vines and other staples in your decorations. Apple topiaries or baskets filled with flowers look mouth-watering or you can fill glass vases with tiny crab apples and top with a mixed seasonal hand-tie for a loose country feel.

If you are looking for autumn scent use late-flowering garden roses or herbs in your arrangements. I love to use angelica and the fragrant fronds of dill. Flowering mint and marjoram will also add scent and colour to fall table centres.

ABOVE Daisies are a classic choice for a country wedding. The chrysanthemums used here (*Chrysanthemum* 'Reagan White') are available all year round. They are arranged in a terracotta pot with a rope handle, making this an easy display for a small bridesmaid to carry, and put down when necessary.

BELOW, CLOCKWISE FROM TOP RIGHT
Late summer- or autumn-flowering chocolate cosmos are an unusual, but striking, bridal flower as they are quite difficult to acquire; Fruit and vegetables can be used at any time of year to add colour and texture to your flower arrangements. Here a savoy cabbage has been filled with iceberg roses for a simple table centre; Red and orange flowers are more popular in the autumn and winter months. Here red nerines are mixed with open roses, pincushion proteas, berries and hips to create a spectacular and colourful candelabra.

winter

Wintertime brings a new range of flowers for the bride to use. Rich colours appeal to our senses and traditional rich fare is fuel for our bodies. One winter special is *Euphorbia fulgens*, which is an arched stem of many tiny florets. It is related to poinsettias and oozes a milky sap that can be an irritant to your skin, so be careful when using it or wear protective gloves. These delicate flowers are great in vase arrangements and pedestals as they give a lovely trail to the overall shape. Cymbidiums are at their best in the winter months and the large varieties work well in huge pedestal arrangements. The florets make great corsages for wrists or handbags, and the mini cymbidiums are ideal for wiring into headdresses. Cymbidium orchids are very long last-

ing and versatile. They last well out of water and so the flower heads can be scattered on a table with votives or wired into twiggy wreathes to add colour. Their range of colour is immense and the new burgundy and brown varieties are most intriguing. A personal favourite of mine is lime green with burgundy blooms and I love to mix this with deep 'Black Baccara' roses and interesting foliage for a striking effect.

Of course a winter wedding is all about using the rich evergreen foliage, such as ivy, mistletoe and spruce, that has always held a special significance for us because of its association with fidelity and fertility. These plants are very aromatic and the use of spruce and eucalyptus in your wedding decorations will also give the ceremony a very fresh and clean scent as well as a seasonal look.

Spring flowers also start to come back on the scene and so tulips, ranunculus, anemones and hyacinths are available again. Amaryllis are an option now too and these look stunning in large arrangements and also cut up as table decorations. If you want to use them potted they work well lined up on

mantelpieces and in church windows surrounded by a mass of candles and votives. One of my favourite festive arrangements with amaryllis is to use it bunched as a topiary tree set on a flat dish and anchored by a pin holder or packed into low pots filled with floral foam.

There are also some fantastic berries and seed heads on offer in winter and one of my favourites is skimmia — both in its berried form and used as flowering stems. Eucalyptus is great too and the grey seed heads add a touch of festive silver to any bunch. Ilex berries in red and yellow also add a splash of bright colour to large groupings of flowers. Alternatively, of course, roses are still very much available and are an excellent source of rich colour. In winter they are often used in red or white arrangements to great effect along with gerberas and chrysanthemums, which are available all the year round.

spring wedding

planning a wedding takes a lot of organisation, and the process was even more complicated for Monica and John, who were living and working in Asia and marrying in England. They were making arrangements from a long distance and in a different time zone. After a few frantic visits back home to get things under way they decided to appoint a wedding planner, Sophie Lillingstone, to advise them and take care of all the arrangements for the day, giving them peace of mind to enjoy their wedding.

As their ceremony took place in spring, we were able to use fresh growth from deciduous trees (including sorbus and beech) in the decorations. We combined this with masses of freshly grown fragrant herbs mixed with peonies, the first garden roses and sweet peas. For the ceremony, Monica chose a white-and-cream colour scheme to stand out in the grand marble interior of her venue and to match the bridal-party flowers. She decided on stephanotis pips as buttonholes for the bridegroom and his groomsmen and her attendants also wore this flower. The three adult bridesmaids wore it in their headdresses while the three flower girls had stephanotis pips incorporated into their decorations. They also held beautifully scented posies of sweet peas combined with *Viburnum opulus*. For her own bouquet, Monica chose to carry a beautiful posy of white peonies edged with hosta leaves.

For their reception they chose to use more vibrant blues and pinks to soften the interior of the venue and fill it with scent. For the entrance we created an arch by placing two pedestals either side of a corridor and using long branches of foliage to meet in the middle. As the ballroom was on the first floor, garlands of ivy and roses were arranged all the way along the bannisters to invite the guests upstairs. Mantelpieces are perfect for floral decorations as they are exactly the right height to brighten the room. We decorated one with a formal front-facing arrangement and another with lots of round pots of rosemary, filled with roses, sweet peas and masses of twinkling nightlights. Rosemary became the dominant theme for the table arrangements. We used a mix of high and low displays on the tables. As they were so narrow (only 60 centimetres across) we chose tall fluted vases and filled these with rosemary, topped with herbs, roses and peonies with a collar of ivy wrapped around them. The low-level arrangements were created by covering glass tumblers with rosemary and hand-tying small posies of butterfly lavender, astrantia, roses and sweet peas. Pillar candles were encircled with rosemary and each guest had a small posy of thyme, mint, lavender and rosemary tied with raffia on their napkin.

ABOVE White peonies are readily available for about six weeks in the middle of the year and are the quintessential bouquet flower. The bridegroom and the groomsmen all wore scented pips of stephanotis for their buttonholes.
LEFT Monica chose to use white and green for the church and her bridal flowers. This is quite a traditional choice and often most complementary for dark church interiors. The bridesmaids and flower girls are clutching posies of white sweet peas mixed with *Viburnum opulus*.

ABOVE LEFT The white theme is picked up in the classic cars, which have been decorated with ribbons. **ABOVE RIGHT** A simple hand-tied bouquet of *Viburnum opulus* and white sweet peas, to be carried by one of the bridesmaids. It's advisable to put bouquets like this in water during the reception to prevent them from drooping. **LEFT** Heavy marble interiors found in many religious buildings suit grand arrangements. White and cream often show up best being more noticeable than mixed colours or dark shades, such as blue, purple and burgundy. This arrangement includes spring branches mixed with delphiniums, stocks and lilies.

"It is the art of a great florist to decorate a space and create an atmosphere that is a true reflection of the couple. Paula achieved this to perfection – they were over the moon!" SOPHIE

ABOVE LEFT White peonies are here edged with seasonal hosta leaves. If you are choosing white wedding flowers and wearing an ivory gown, an edging of leaves separates the flowers from the colour of the fabric. **ABOVE** Two pedestals have been placed on either side of a corridor to create the effect of an arch. The tall branches of white-leaf foliage (sorbus) have been used to join in the centre asymmetrically. Grand flower arrangements such as these are best created *in situ* so that the flowers are designed to fit the space. Blue 'Harlequin' delphiniums give height to the arrangement while the lilies (*Lilium* 'Sissi') create a welcoming scent. **LEFT** The mantelpiece is the perfect place for a contrasting display. **OPPOSITE (CLOCKWISE FROM TOP LEFT)** Occasional-table arrangements featuring cut rosemary round a glass tumbler are filled with a rose-and-herb posy; Tall fluted glass vases are filled with rosemary and topped with a posy of hand-tied roses and herbs; Each napkin is decorated with herbs tied with raffia; A stair-case garland marks the route for the guests.

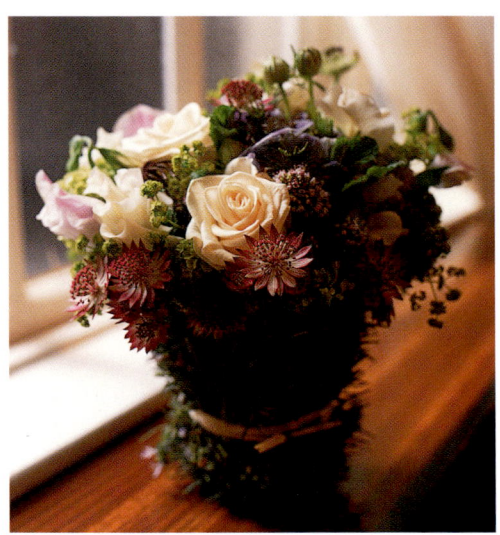

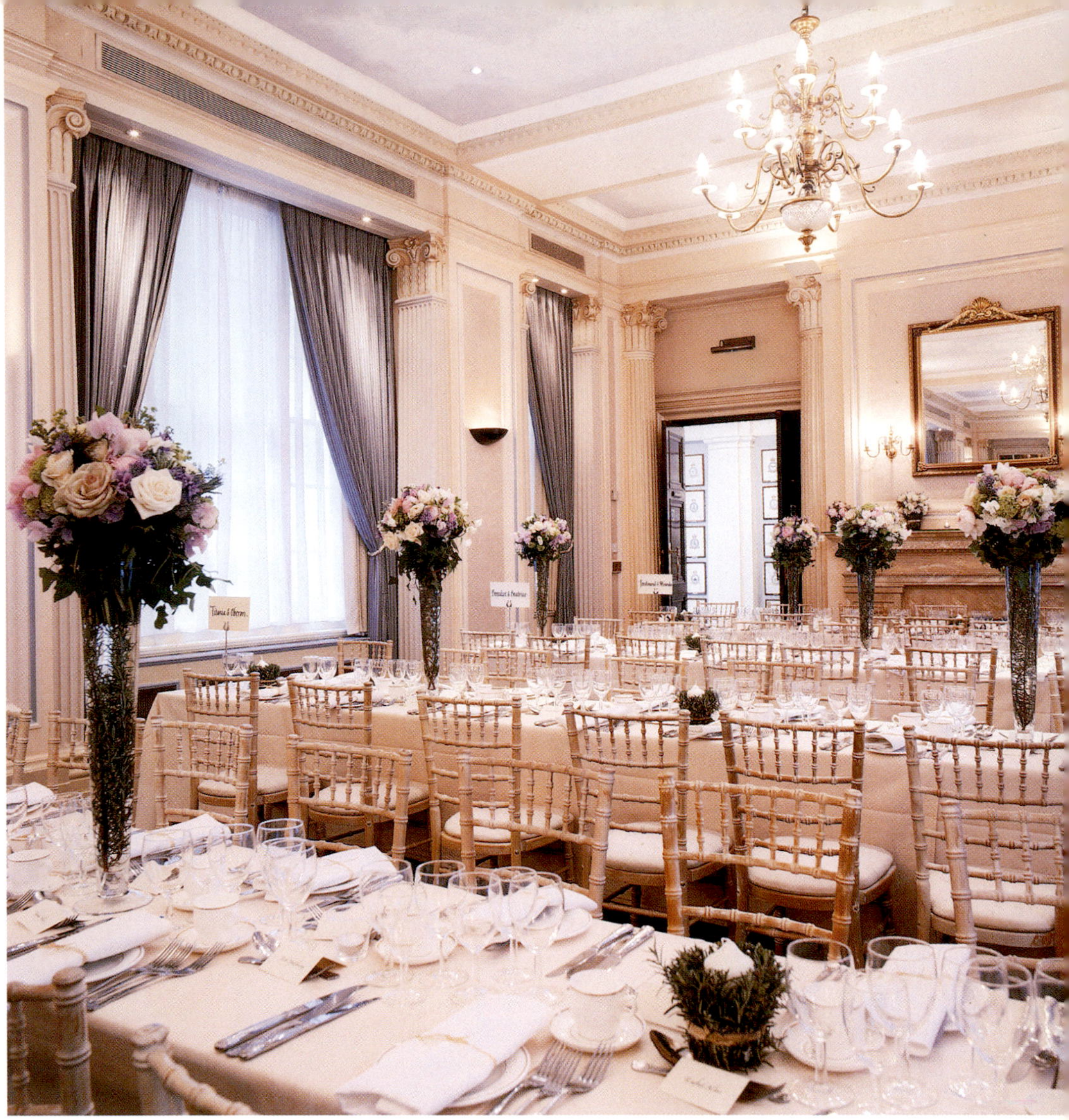

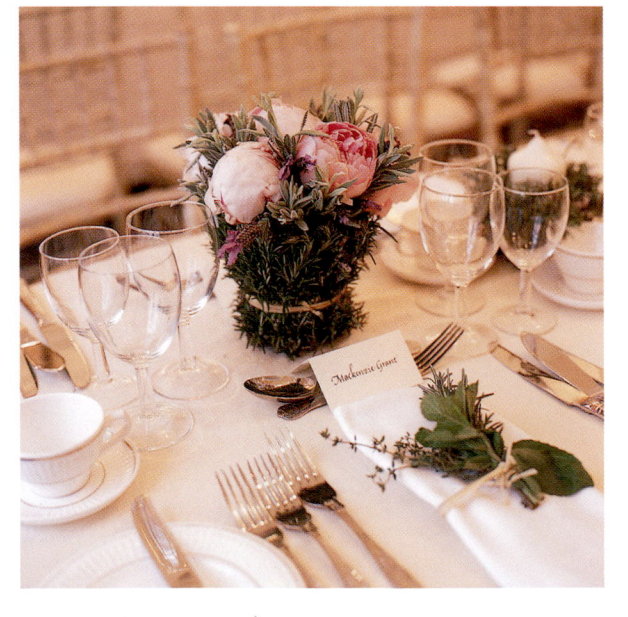

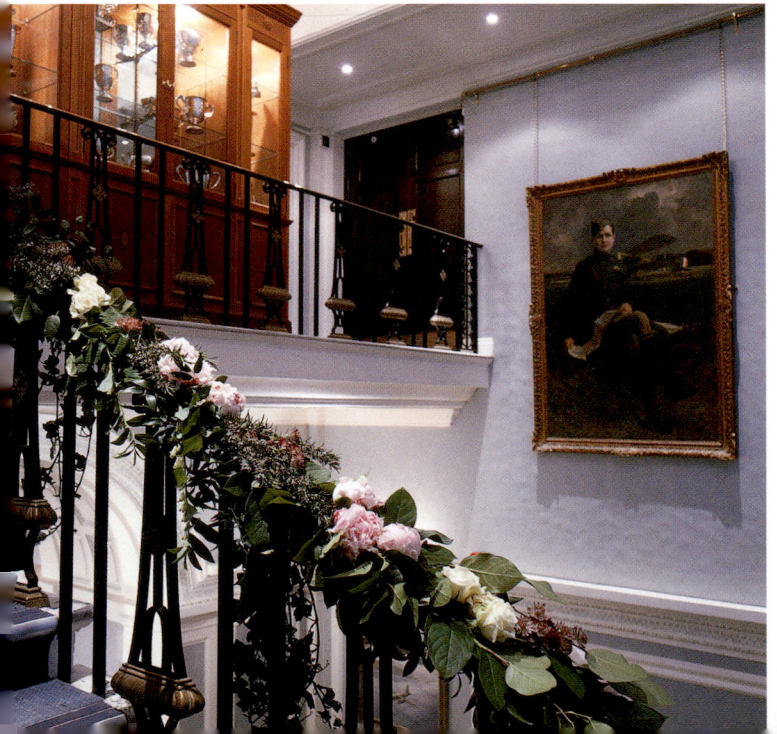

summer wedding

an informal, country wedding

is the ideal occasion for romantic summer flowers. Julie's marriage to Fred is a perfect example. The wedding was held at a local church with the reception in a huge marquee on the family's farm. As soon as Julie and Fred announced their engagement, Julie's father and brother started work levelling out part of a field and re-sowing the grass so that they could pitch a marquee overlooking the picturesque valley where Julie had grown up. It was no coincidence that Julie, who manages a farm office, picked late summer for her wedding, once the harvest was over. As she is passionate about flowers, we knew that she would want to include lots of floral arrangements in her wedding scheme. She chose to incorporate some of the wild flowers grown on her farm, such as rushes and hops as well as some cultivated wheat in her arrangements. Country weddings suit colour and as Julie had chosen lilac for her bridesmaids' dresses, a blue-and-lilac theme soon started to emerge.

It was a real rural affair: many of the villagers came to see Julie at the church, and the couple rode their horses from the church to the reception. Julie practised riding side-saddle with a blanket to see if she could cope with her bridal gown and on the day the couple made this romantic trip together with friends and family following on foot for the short journey from church to marquee.

Julie cut some long vines of hops which we bound with wire. We added bunches of wheat and then open, white lilies and bright blue hydrangea heads. Arches can be difficult to construct as there are often no fixings in the walls to anchor the greenery and flowers. Julie's church benefitted by having a central light to which we could attach the wire, and there were also some metal fixings around the edge of the door that we were able to use. It is important to check what is allowed in the venue when you are planning your ceremony, before deciding on any decorations that may not be practical or permitted.

We lined the aisle with metal candelabras containing thick round candles, and round rings of flowers in a blue-and-white theme using lilies, hydrangeas and roses along with lots of trailing ivies. Two large terracotta amphoras were set at the top of the aisle, on either side of the altar, and a huge spray of flowers was arranged along the altar table. To set the scene, votives were lit in all the church windows and trailing flower arrangements were placed on any available window surface.

OPPOSITE Julie and Fred pose for photographs beneath the floral arch, which was created using hops bound together, with sheaves of wheat tied on. We added hydrangea heads and open 'Casa Blanca' lilies. BELOW When the pews are not suitable for pew ends or when you wish to add some candlelight, free-standing candelabras lining the pews are a nice idea. These chunky candelabras were created using a small floral foam wreath frame placed on top of the candelabra and filled with groups of hydrangeas, lilies and roses. RIGHT The choice of colours for the flowers for Julie's wedding was inspired by her choice of fabric for the bridesmaids' dresses – a popular source of inspiration for a theme.

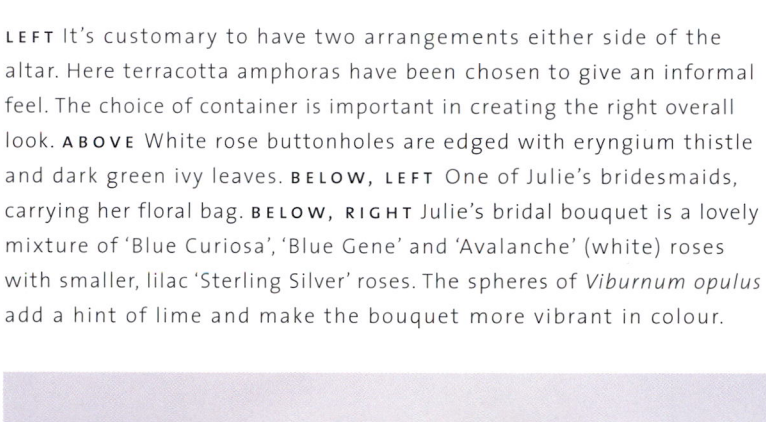

LEFT It's customary to have two arrangements either side of the altar. Here terracotta amphoras have been chosen to give an informal feel. The choice of container is important in creating the right overall look. ABOVE White rose buttonholes are edged with eryngium thistle and dark green ivy leaves. BELOW, LEFT One of Julie's bridesmaids, carrying her floral bag. BELOW, RIGHT Julie's bridal bouquet is a lovely mixture of 'Blue Curiosa', 'Blue Gene' and 'Avalanche' (white) roses with smaller, lilac 'Sterling Silver' roses. The spheres of *Viburnum opulus* add a hint of lime and make the bouquet more vibrant in colour.

"When I walked into the church I was completely overwhelmed by how it had been transformed in such a short time. The flowers in the marquee were fantastic too!" JULIE

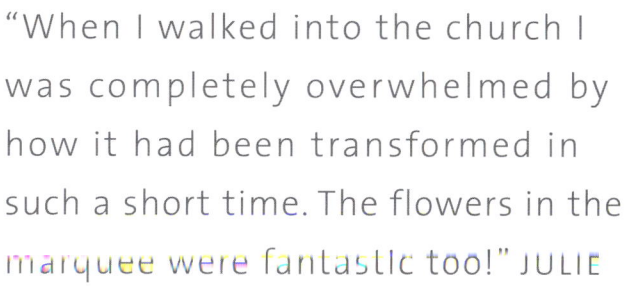

TOP LEFT The happy bridal party line up for the family photos outside the church. The bridesmaids' hair and bouquets are trimmed with the same co-ordinating organza ribbon. **TOP RIGHT** One of the bridesmaids' bags filled with 'Blue Curiosa' roses. The roses are hand-tied and then aqua-packed into the bag so they have a supply of water but are light to carry. **LEFT** The Lady Chapel decked with vases, candles and trailing window arrangements surrounded by many votives.

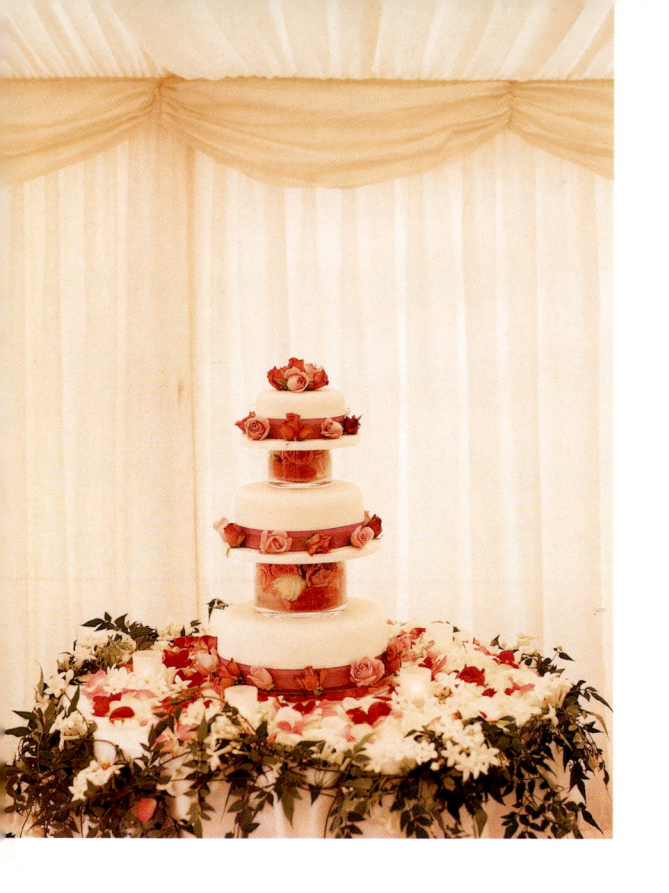

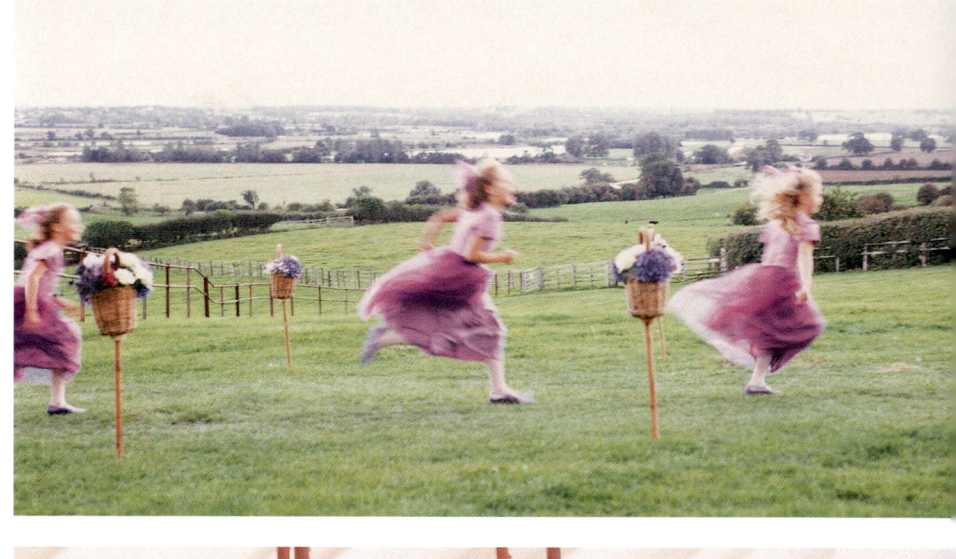

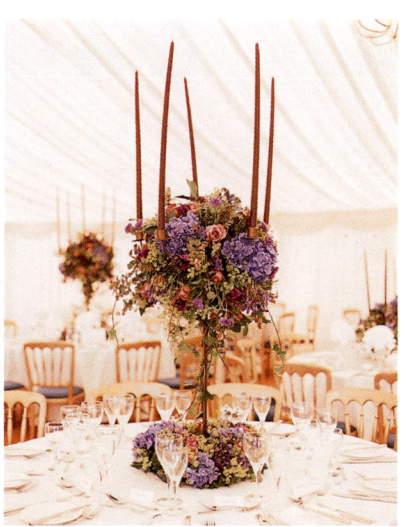

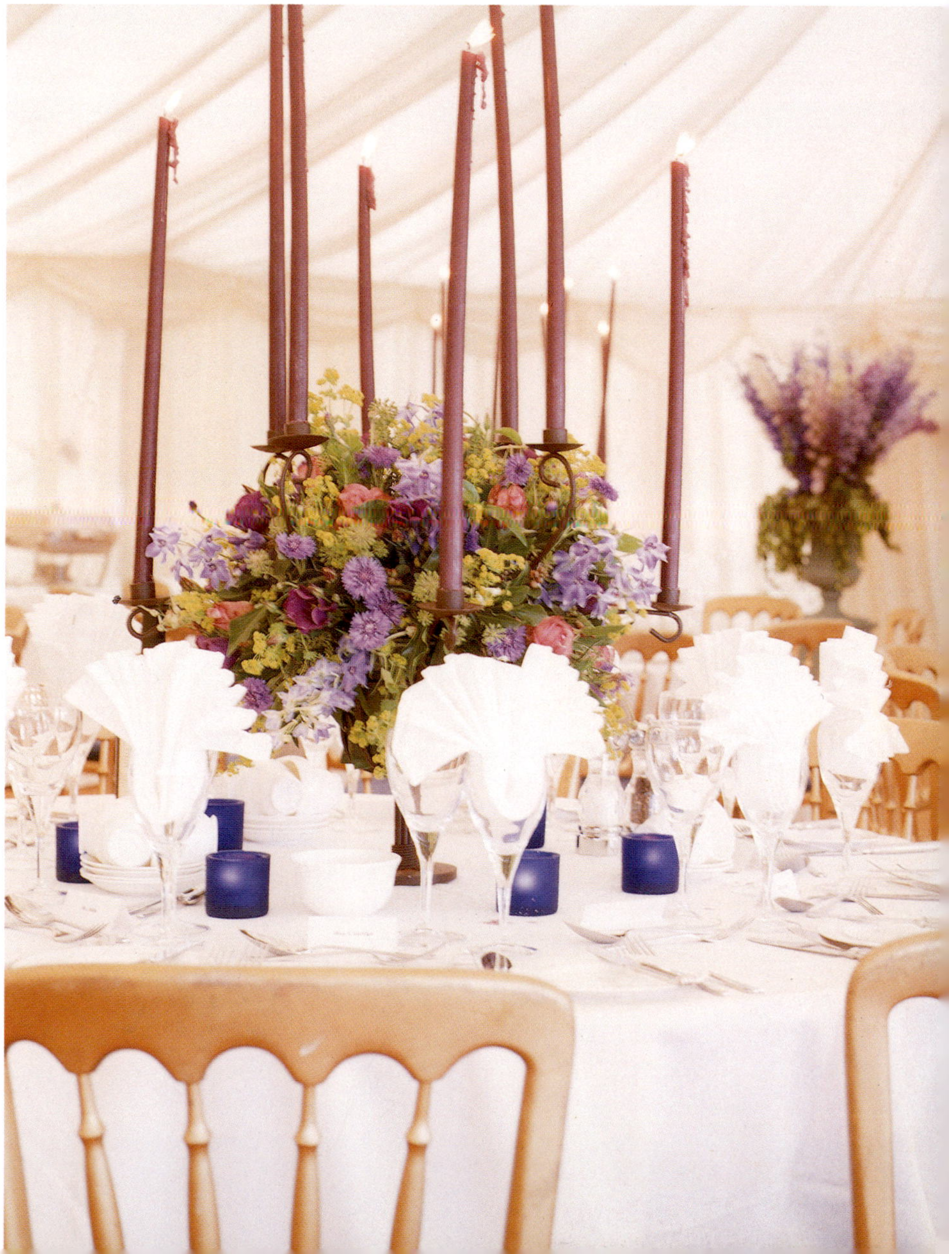

FAR LEFT, TOP Sprays of fragrant stephanotis and masses of rose petals and frosted nightlights add the finishing touch to the cake. OPPOSITE, TOP RIGHT Julie's bridesmaids run across from the field from the marquee to her home, through a path of mushroom baskets filled with hydrangeas and roses. FAR LEFT Classic candelabras always look elegant at a reception. Usually we arrange flowers at the top and in a ring at the base allowing the guests to see across the table. LEFT The candelabras are filled with seasonal blue flowers – cornflowers, veronica, garden roses, sweet peas and hydrangeas. Urns of blue hydrangea and ivy are also used to decorate the huge marquee. ABOVE The bridesmaids' bouquets are smaller versions of Julie's bouquet with sweet peas as well roses. RIGHT Mushroom baskets are a lovely way to mark out a patch in a beautiful rural setting like this. The baskets have been lined with plastic and filled with floral foam and flowers.

autumn wedding

rich, warm colours are perfect for an autumn wedding – and Bella and Nick used just such a theme for their special day. They chose to celebrate it at two alternative venues. As they wanted to involve their treasured dog in the ceremony they needed to find two locations that were fairly relaxed about this. Bella had often attended lectures at The Royal Geographical Society and discovered that, with their own dog in permanent residence, they were happy to allow Pip to act as bridesmaid for the civil ceremony. The wedding party travelled to the reception in an old-fashioned bus and each guest was given a hand-embroidered bag filled with bottles of chilled champagne and smoked almonds to fuel the celebration by Nick's 'bus conductors'. For their reception, Nick and Bella chose an historic period property that has retained most of its original features and has been lovingly restored by its owners, who often hire it out to television companies as a setting for period dramas.

Bella is a discerning flower lover who had recently edited a book on herbs, so together we made an early morning trip to a local flower market where we decided that the floral arrangements would have a fragrant herbal theme throughout. Bella also decided to make the most of the early autumnal blooms and foliage, and wanted the overall effect to include native plants. She decided that her

Paul Smith dress would perfectly suit a round bouquet of chocolate cosmos and I kept my fingers crossed hoping there would be some available for her. They are available in scant quantities from late summer and I feared that October would be too late. The fragile beauty of their stems and the fact they smell divinely of rich chocolate add to their attraction. We settled on an alternative of late garden roses in case cosmos did prove to be unavailable. (If you set your heart on a particular flower, especially an uncommon one, it is a good idea to have an alternative in mind to avoid disappointment.)

At the reception aromatic herbs including myrtle were woven into garlands and hung on the staircases. Loosely arranged herbs such as dill and garden roses were placed in simple earthernware jugs. Bella had also picked huge quantities of lavender and rosemary from her mother's country garden and every old oak floor in the house was strewn with them, so that as the guests moved around the house the herbs released their familiar fragrance. Hop vines from Kent garlanded the bar table and were twisted around pillars in the main reception room, while jugs of fever-few daisies decorated the trestle tables.

"As we stepped inside the house on that cool October evening, the room was filled with the welcoming aroma of herbs and old-fashioned roses. It was everything that we dreamed it would be." BELLA

OPPOSITE Bella sits with her delicious posy of chocolate cosmos. The deep velvet texture of cosmos and the delectable colour (not quite brown and not quite burgundy) make these flowers a real treasure. LEFT Bella wore a Paul Smith dress decorated with roses, which are one of her favourite flowers and were part of the theme throughout the celebration. ABOVE The elegant Pip in the silk ruff that Bella had made by jewellery designer Heidi Sturgess. BELOW, LEFT AND RIGHT Breaking with convention, Bella and Nick leave for the wedding ceremony together in a plum-coloured Karma Cab. The bumpers are decorated with brightly coloured *faux* flowers and the interior echoes the exotic theme. Both complement the flowers on Bella's dress.

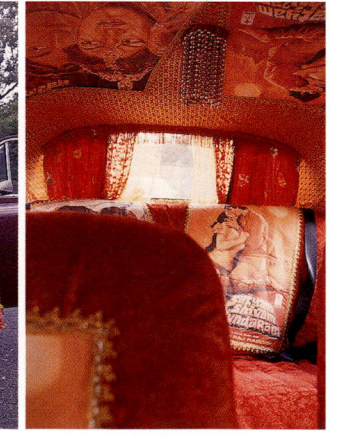

RIGHT This herb garland is made from bay, rosemary, sage and thyme with a touch of scented eucalyptus, trailing ivy and eryngium thistle. The foliage is bound onto a rope using a heavy blue reel wire. The garland is secured to the handrail of the staircase with string. **BELOW** Galvanised buckets of herbs and old-fashioned roses, loosely arranged, are a feature in every room of the house. **BELOW RIGHT** Earthenware pots are filled with 'Black Baccara' and 'Xtreme' roses, flowering mint, dill and ivy, to great effect.

ABOVE Bella and Nick share a moment together after the ceremony. They brought back dried rose petals from a trip to Morocco and scattered these at the venue. Baskets of petals were also offered to guests to throw as confetti, when they left the building.
TOP RIGHT An earthenware pot containing scented roses, sage, dill, rosemary and mint welcomes the guests at the front door. **RIGHT** For this historic home antique galvanised buckets and earthenware pots are perfect for the floral arrangements. They suit the interior and match Bella and Nick's vision for the day.

winter wedding

a cosy and warm winter wedding

brought together Jane's English family with Ewan's clan from Scotland. Traditional Scottish wedding dress and Scottish dancing gave the wedding a flavour of the north, while their choice of venues gave it a sophisticated urban feel. (Jane and Ewan chose to hold their ceremony in a Catholic church in the city centre, and decided on a nearby club for the reception.)

For the church decorations Jane worked with the church florist to create large arrangements in her chosen scheme of bright red and lime greens. Rich green foliage is perfect for a winter wedding and, mixed with red and green blooms in this way, produces a warm and festive theme. (Some churches are strict about who they allow to decorate and arrange flowers for ceremonies and many have a team of flower arrangers who like to be involved in the wedding decorations. Check with the priest or vicar about the protocol in your chosen church.)

For the reception Jane and Ewan chose a venue which happened to be decorated in a very rich red. As Jane loves 'Grand Prix' roses she developed a floral scheme around these, to complement the décor, including rich green celosia, green and red cymbidium orchids and long red Singapore orchids. All the arrangements followed this luxurious festive theme, echoing the displays that were created for the church.

The table decorations were created in two heights, with half being high candelabras containing chunky square candles and half being low square arrangements around huge square five-wick candles, giving a romantic feel to the reception. The tall arrangements were constructed by binding hebe to heavy metal candelabras so that the candelabra looked like a living topiary. Floral foam was added to the top and the striking 'Liberty' and 'Grand Prix' roses, along with amaryllis, celosia, Singapore orchids and cymbidium were added in groups. A ring of flowers was added to the base to conceal the heavy metal plate.

The lower arrangements were constructed using a square of designer board that was cut to give a 5-centimetre edge of foam around the candle. Groups of 'Liberty' and 'Grand Prix' roses, amaryllis, celosia, Singapore orchids and cymbidium were added with hebe and ivy berries completing the seasonal theme. In addition to the table arrangements, floral displays for the bar and other vases around the venue followed the same scheme.

LEFT Jane and Ewan leaving the church after signing the register. Jane carries a simply tied bouquet of phalaenopsis orchids. **ABOVE** Ewan wears traditional Scottish dress – a Hunting Ogilvy tartan kilt with kilt pin, cream socks with green flashes and his Sgain Dubh (stocking knife).

LEFT These tall candelabras, covered in hebe and topped with roses and orchids, don't prevent conversation across the table as the stem is thin. Candlelight is very flattering and adds to the ambience of any party. **ABOVE RIGHT** The best man, guiding the guests and checking on his notes for the speech. Like Ewan, the groomsmen wore traditional Scottish dress. **BELOW LEFT** Jane and Ewan have a moment to reflect in the park under the autumn trees. The phalaenopsis orchids in Jane's hair have been wired individually and positioned by Jane's hairdresser. **BELOW RIGHT** Flared-footed glass vases of red and green, including the trailing *Euphorbia fulgens* are super for winter weddings.

"We couldn't have asked for anything more beautiful than the sight of our family and friends surrounded by the warm glow of candlelight and masses of incredible velvety roses." JANE

winter wedding

an intimate breakfast

an intimate breakfast shared with a small number of invited guests was the special choice of gourmets Shelly-Ann and Stuart for their wedding. They picked Raymond Blanc's restaurant, Le Manoir aux Quat' Saisons, as a venue – not only for its fabulous food and renowned hospitality, but also its accessibility.

Shelly-Ann's family originally came from Trinidad and she wanted to reflect her ancestry in her wedding flowers, at the same time keeping the decorations very contemporary and smart. Shelly-Ann's personal preference for a simple, elegant look is reflected both in her stunning dress and the floral arrangements, and this consistent reflection of the bride's individuality is key to a successful theme. Shelly-Ann loves white calla lilies and green orchids and anthuriums, so a cool white-and-green theme using lots of exotic fruits and foliage became the look of their very individual wedding. Kentia palm, monstera and anthurium leaves mixed with phormium, papyrus and trailing date palms added texture and shape to the arrangements. Star fruit and lime kumquats were used throughout the table arrangements and pillar candles were covered with equisetum to give the table a lush tropical effect. Large cube vases were lined with flax, while white calla lilies, cymbidium orchids and date palm created a sumptuous feel, and reflected the choice of flowers of the bridal party. Both Stuart and Shelly-Ann liked the effect of using fruits in glass containers and this seemed appropriate for their gourmet setting. Glass is extremely versatile and and can be used in many ways to suit classic or modern receptions. Slip covers were carefully chosen to match the table linen and finish the elegant look in the dining room. Le Manoir has lovely gardens and the private rooms where the ceremony and dinner were to be held were entered through two stone columns presenting the perfect place to arrange two garlands in the white-and-green theme with more tropical foliage.

Once inside the private rooms Stuart and Shelly-Ann wanted to create a more sensual ambience with candlelight and lots of tropical fruits and flowers in huge flared vases, such as red alpinia gingers flown in from Trinidad, equisetum, monstera leaves and brush papyrus. The romantic lighting and lush floral decoration brought a warmth to the ceremony in perfect contrast to the crisp winter weather.

LEFT The bridegroom, looking very handsome in his Oswald Boateng purple suit, strides up to the ceremony accompanied by guests attired in traditional Scottish costume.
ABOVE Shelly-Ann chose a simple Vera Wang dress. As she is very tall, she decided a simply tied over-the-arm bouquet of white calla lilies most suited her style and gown, and created an elegant look.

ABOVE LEFT Cymbidium orchids were given to each guest to wear for the day. **ABOVE CENTRE** Alpinia gingers edged with papyrus and monstera leaves in a vase lined with snake grass make a sleek pedestal for the intimate ceremony. **ABOVE RIGHT** The groom's formal dress matches the exclusive venue and Shelly-Ann's elegant look. **LEFT** The columns of the private dining area have ridges which make them perfect for arranging collars of flowers. Kentia palm leaves and flax are woven through the design, created on floral foam racks, to enhance the circular look. **BELOW** Trailing arrangements for the celebrants' top table include striped fronds of date palm.

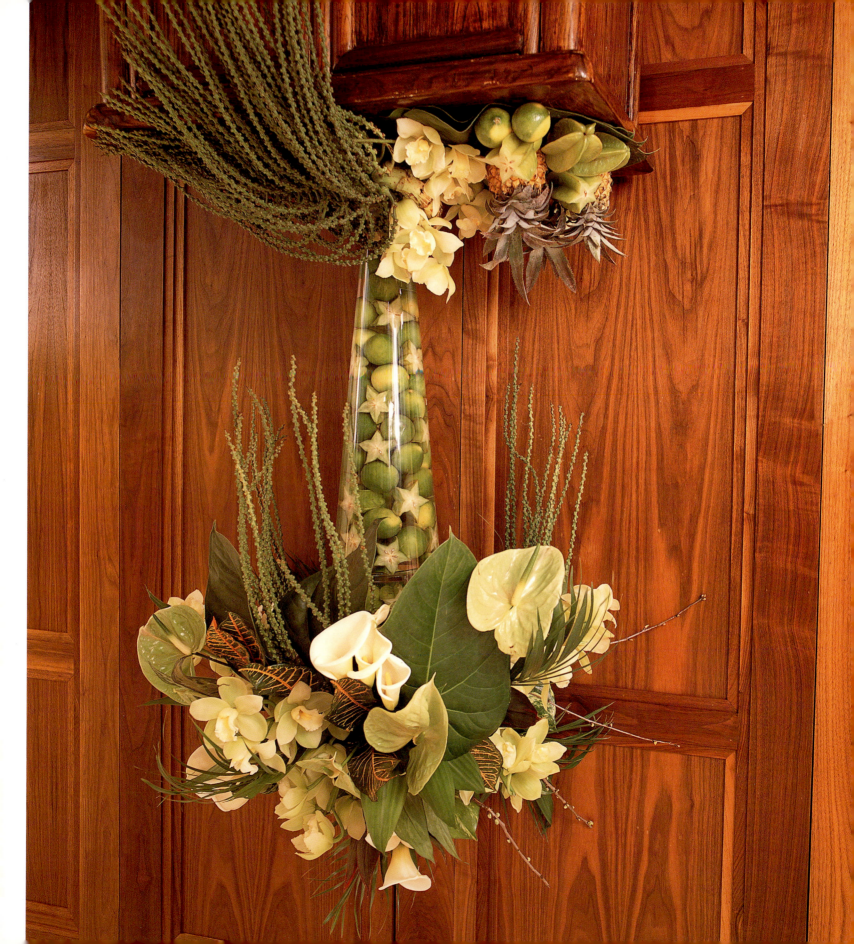

OPPOSITE The reception arrangements for the wedding breakfast were filled with lime kumquats and topped with 'Midori' anthuriums, white calla lilies, slipper and cymbidium orchids, and rich tropical foliage. LEFT Elegant slip covers matching the table cloth always make a room look very smart and bridal. Three cube vases were placed down the centre of a long oblong table and candles covered in snake grass and masses of votives were dotted along the centre of the dining table. BELOW LEFT Flax and calla lilies mixed with a 'Midori' anthurium and date palms make this a perfect chairback to suit the theme. BELOW RIGHT The bridal party pose for pictures.

"The floral arrangements were, without doubt, the highlight of our day. They created exactly the sensual ambience we had hoped to achieve during the ceremony, which was really magical." STUART

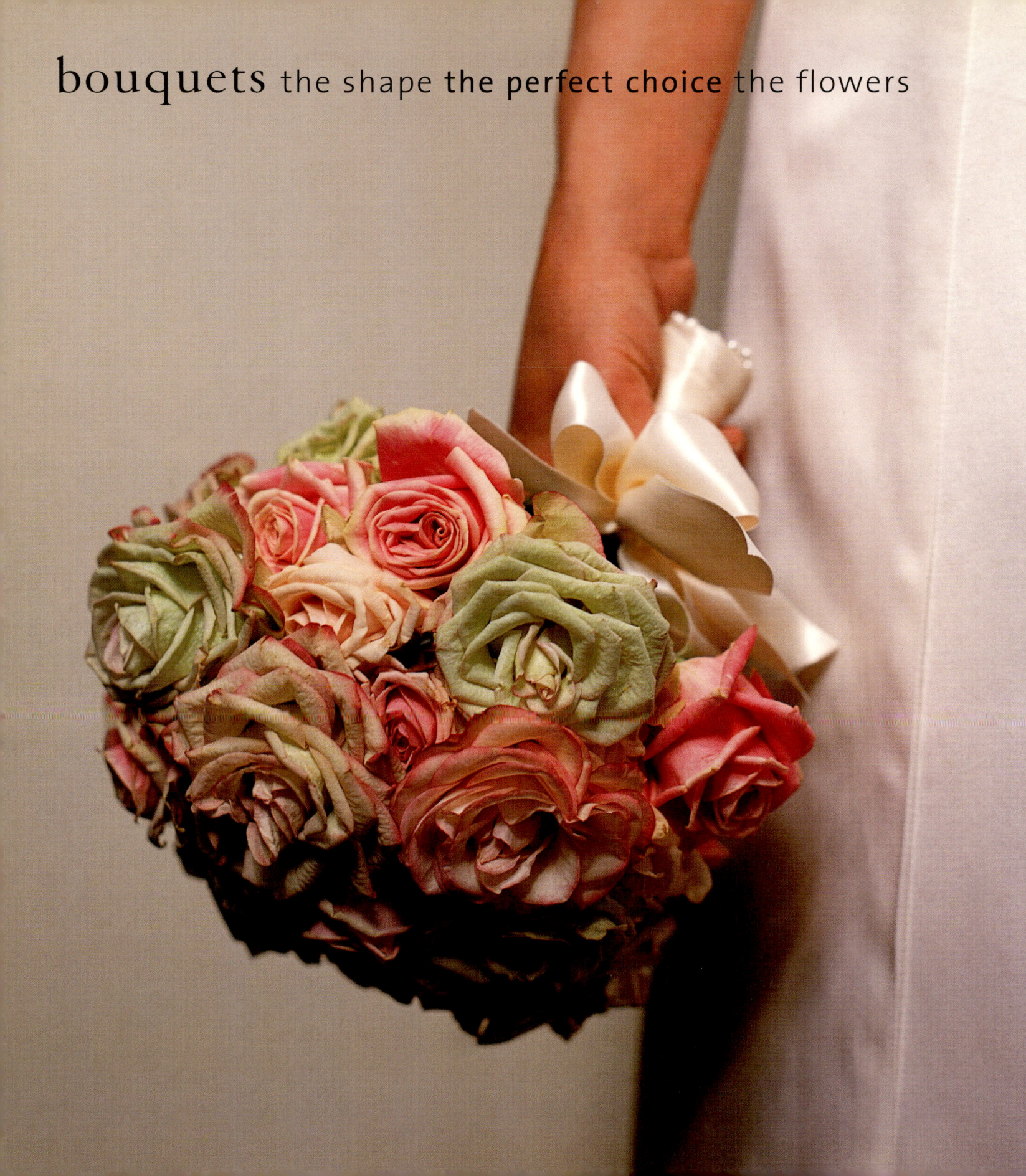

bouquets the shape **the perfect choice** the flowers

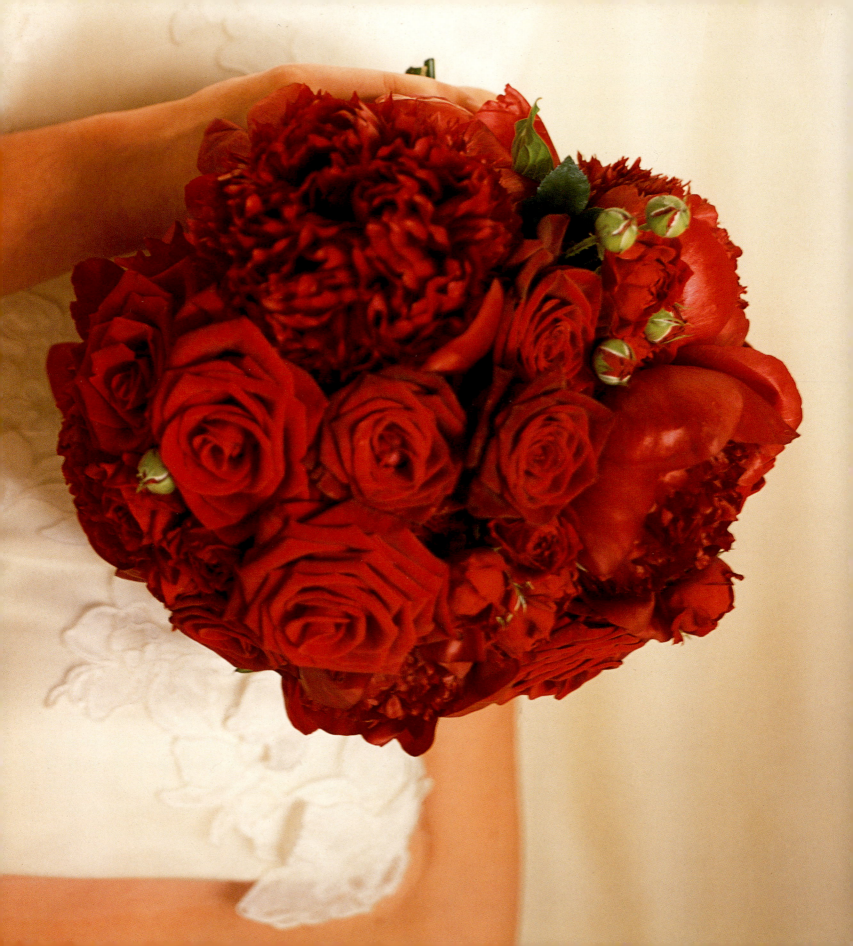

Fresh flowers enhance your wedding in every way but the one floral accessory everyone will remember is the bride's bouquet. Choosing the flowers for your bouquet will be one of the most pleasant pre-wedding tasks you will have to perform. You should be able to work with your florist to create a unique bouquet that is perfect for you and that you will feel comfortable carrying to your ceremony. It will be the most photographed floral arrangement on the day and it should complement you and your chosen gown in every way.

Bridal bouquets began in medieval times as a small nosegay of sweetly scented flowers. Over the years they have changed and expanded but only became a wedding essential in Victorian times. The growth of the floristry business and the development of the skills of individual florists have in the last century meant that you can have a bouquet fashioned into just about any shape you like. Each flower head can be individually wired and the shape re-constructed. The bouquet can take the form of a half moon, a curved pear, a heart or even a letter of the alphabet. Wiring flowers also makes them lighter and the handle of the bouquet will be thinner and neater in most cases. It can often be advantageous for the bride to request a wired bouquet. A heavy bouquet can become uncomfortable over the length of the wedding day.

By far the most common shape for a bouquet, however, is the tear-shaped cascade bouquet or shower. Although these are generally thought to be quite traditional there are ways of making them contemporary and, in the hands of a skilled florist, these bouquets can become very individual and imaginative. If you require a shower or cascade bouquet it is possible to have the flowers bound with their natural stems but sometimes it is best to have them wired together. There are two main reasons for this. Some flowers are simply too short and need to be wired to gain the extra length required. Others are too fragile and they will last better if they are wired and taped into place.

choosing the flowers
There are no hard-and-fast rules about wedding flowers and it really is down to your own personal taste as to what you decide to choose. In recent years there has been a trend for a simple round hand-tied bouquet on natural stems, usually of the same coloured roses tied with a matching ribbon. (The wedding press has inadvertently made this fashionable by commissioning a number of these bouquets from florists.) The advantage is that they are relatively easy and quick to create and always photograph well however they are held!

The natural, just-picked collection of flowers has also been popular as well as the inclusion of herbs in a bouquet using favourites such as lavender, rosemary, sage, lemon balm, myrtle and scented eucalyptus.

Choosing which flowers to have in your bridal bouquet is extremely personal. Some brides have flowers that are symbolic of their relationship with their husband-to-be. Brides wearing antique dresses or family heirlooms very often wish to style a

bouquet from their family album and may even bring in a family portrait from which to take inspiration. To get an insight into the bouquet that you think you might be comfortable holding it is a good idea to browse through wedding magazines and books and look for ideas that appeal. After some time you should start to build up an idea of the design you like and it will be easier to discuss this with your florist if you use the help of clippings – particularly as most people's botanical knowledge is limited!

colour

Of course the overwhelming majority of brides now choose to get married in white but this was not always the case. This particular custom only became popular in the Victorian period. If your dress is white or ivory, whether you choose white or a colour for your flowers may depend on what kind of look you are trying to create. If you are planning a really formal wedding you will probably plump for an all-white bouquet of one type of flower or a combination. You may decide to pick one of the more traditional flowers: lily-of-the-valley, gardenias, stephanotis, peonies, freesias, calla lilies, tulips, orchids and – of course – roses.

If you do decide to choose white then there is an enormous range of shades within this one colour. The whitest blooms are phalaenopsis orchids. Sweet peas and 'Akito' roses, gardenias and calla lilies can be quite creamy. White does always look sophisticated and is the most traditional choice. It is also symbolic of purity and the lily in particular symbolises innocence. Brides marrying for the second time may therefore shy away from this choice of flower. Some brides worry that white flowers on white fabric will be lost but most bouquets are edged with foliage that lifts them from the dress material. Unsurprisingly most dress designers, if asked, would recommend white flowers as this often shows off their dresses to the best advantage! They often advise using delicate bouquets for the same reason.

Some brides feel uncomfortable at the thought of wearing all white and carrying white flowers, and prefer to pick a pale or pastel colour. They can also pick this up in their make-up and nail varnish. It is true that if you have a very colourful bouquet the eye will be drawn to the flowers. So if you are a 'shrinking violet' and nervous of being the centre of attention then choose a vibrant collection of flowers for your bouquet.

If you have chosen to wear a colour other than white this will obviously affect your choice too. (From a very young age I always saw myself in a pink gown. As the old rhyme says "Married in pink, of you he will always think!") But in the end I opted for the traditional ivory using the flowers to emphasise my love of pink. ("Married in white, she

OPPOSITE An informal round bouquet of fragrant summer flowers including *Alchemilla mollis* and gypsophila with 'Blue Moon' and 'Deep Secret' garden roses and sweet peas. **ABOVE (CLOCKWISE FROM TOP LEFT)** A classic, delicate bouquet of white 'Akito' roses combined with scented lily-of-the-valley and edged with lily-of-the-valley leaves; This alternative bouquet of white calla lilies encircled with white ostrich feathers makes a striking contemporary arrangement, which fulfils the bride's fairytale theme and complements her dress; A flamboyant shower bouquet using groups of textural flowers including velvety 'Grand Prix' red roses, poppy seed heads and the balls of *Viburnum opulus*, mixed with the exotic heads of cymbidium orchids and spikes of 'James Storei' Singapore orchids edged with fronds of fern.

the shape of your bouquet

Generally speaking, the shape of your bouquet will largely be determined by your dress style and shape. There are basically three styles of bouquet you can choose from: the round, posy bouquet; the long, trailing shower bouquet; and an over-arm bouquet.

An elaborate dress with a wide skirt and cathedral-length veil suits a flamboyant and large bouquet. Masses of silk taffeta and tulle need a long bouquet of a traditional nature. This is more likely to be wired to get the length and may use many varieties of flowers. A slender cut of dress will suit a more structured, longer and thinner bouquet. Arum lilies, phalaenopsis orchids or even anthuriums are suitable for this style of gown. An empire-line or Victorian-style dress will suit a round posy of one type of flowers, or groups of flowers arranged tightly together. Alternatively, choose a Victorian or Biedermeier posy, made from concentric circles of flowers in co-ordinating colours.

You must also consider your own size. If you are tall you may need a longer-stemmed look for an over-arm bouquet or extra length if you choose a trailing bouquet. If you are petite you may end up looking overwhelmed by a huge armful of flowers and a long shower bouquet may not suit your style of dress.

To assist my brides in choosing their bouquet I often accompany them to one of their earlier dress fittings and take some flowers so we can start to decide what suits the dress best. This also gives the bride a chance to see how different flowers look with the backdrop of the skirt of her gown. It helps to involve your florist in the wedding plans, to give her a chance to see the look you want and to gain insight into your personality and style. Your florist will give you advice based on a number of factors: your stature, colouring and your personality as well as your gown. She will steer you away from impractical ideas and guide you towards flowers that last well.

LEFT This grand, white shower bouquet would suit an extravagant wedding and perfectly suit a full skirt and long train. The gardenia and stephanotis flowers have been wired into this trailing design. Because of the length of time required to create this style of bouquet and the number of perfect flower heads that have been used it is an expensive option to choose. This bouquet not only looks stunning but also has a fabulous scent from both the stephanotis and gardenia, which are often chosen as the key scents for perfume.

ABOVE Recent trends for dinner party weddings have meant that some bridal gowns are more glitzy and can be decorated with beads, jewels and crystals. This beautiful Vera Wang dress has been complemented with rich pink garden roses encircled by *faux* diamonds, which pick up the jewelled theme of the gown. A round bouquet is perfectly suited to this straight skirt.

CLOCKWISE FROM RIGHT Full skirts and long trains suit longer and larger bouquets. Here open 'Shirley Temple' peonies have been hand-tied into a tear-drop shape. Massed flowers of one type have recently been the most popular choice for weddings and are perhaps one of the most successful options because they photograph well; Lace or heavy brocade fabric is often complemented by the use of rich colours or heavily textural flowers. The lace fabric of this beautiful Vera Wang gown contains a rose motif, complemented perfectly by the open petals of a bouquet of mixed garden roses. These opulent flowers suit the very decorative nature of the gown; These innocent-looking daisies (*Gerbera* 'Pinky Eye') perfectly complement the simplicity of this Jackie O-style dress.

the perfect choice

A fabulous bridal bouquet can be created with almost any flower and your options are limited only by your own imagination, the seasonal availability of flowers and the skills of your florist. A truly professional florist works at a number of budget ranges and will be sympathetic to your own personal style, working with you to create the most complementary bouquet for your special day. Often there is one flower that may run through the theme of the wedding and appear in the bride's bouquet, the attendants' bouquets, the buttonholes and even the centrepieces for the reception. If this works out that is fine, but I always advise my brides to go with what suits their dress the best and worry less about co-ordinating all the other floral decorations to the bridal bouquet.

Any colour can be incorporated into a bouquet; often the final choice is based on the bridesmaids' gowns, a colour that is most complementary to the bride, or simply a favourite flower or colour. Other factors that might influence your decision are the time of year when your wedding is taking place and the look you choose for the ceremony – formal or informal, traditional or contemporary.

Once you've decided on the perfect shape and colour scheme for your bouquet, ensure that it co-ordinates perfectly with your gown by using the same fabric to wrap the stem or, alternatively, give a swatch to your florist so that they can trim your bouquet with a ribbon to match your dress. Your florist will also be able to advise you on how to hold your bouquet to show it at its best. Check this in a full-length mirror before you leave home so that you point the flowers towards the photographer and make the most of them in your photographs. A good professional photographer will help you to look your best.

OPPOSITE LEFT A round, natural bouquet of mixed colours like this is very popular for summer brides. Lilac, blue and cream roses have been mixed with *Viburnum opulus*. **OPPOSITE RIGHT** This is a large, round bouquet of open peony blooms, which is very suited to the choice of a formal city venue. **THIS PAGE (CLOCKWISE FROM ABOVE)** Phalaenopsis orchids are a very popular choice for brides who would like to have a trailing bouquet but don't want to have anything too formal or fussy. These long stems of orchids can be simply tied together and come in a variety of colours from magenta pink to cinnamon gold; Compact posies of one type of flower are very easy to hold and are by far the most popular choice of bridal bouquet. Here the chocolate cosmos pick up the detail of the dress; Keeping the stems longer requires the bride to either hold the bouquet upright (bottom right) or over the arm (below), as shown with these two different bouquets featuring calla lilies.

the flowers

The choice of flowers for your bridal bouquet is often one of the hardest decisions to make because it will be your most important accessory and it is essential that it should complement both your dress and your personality. You may choose to use flowers that are symbolic of your relationship or simply your favourite varieties. I think a scented bouquet is lovely; I like to use lily-of-the-valley, stephanotis, garden roses or gardenias.

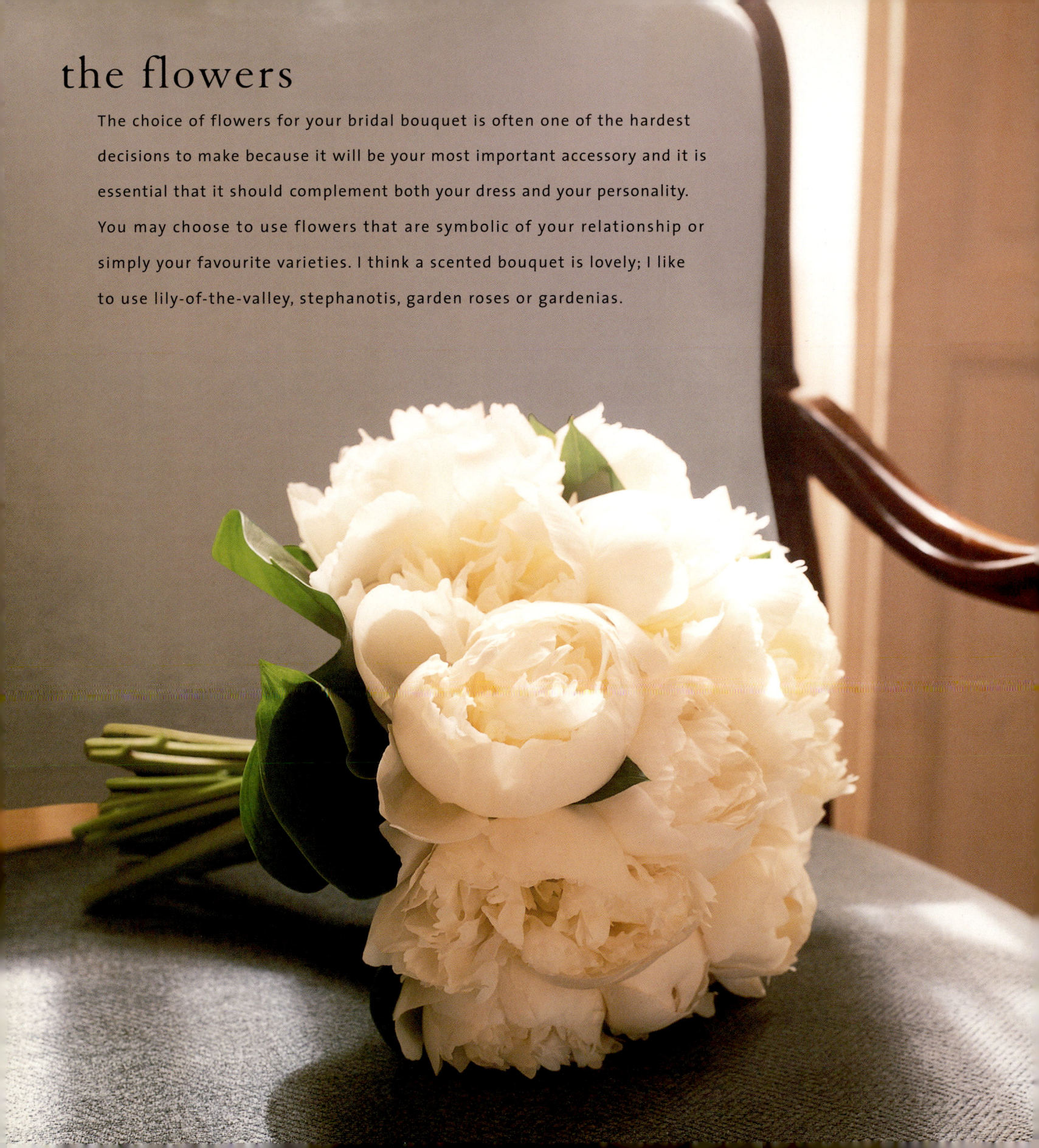

OPPOSITE Fluffy white peonies 'Duchesse de Nemours' hand tied into a simple posy and edged with hosta leaves. **THIS PAGE** A mixed summer bouquet which includes 'Sarah Bernhardt' peonies, pale pink *Astilbe* 'Erica', mock orange *Philadelphus* 'Virginal', double white lisianthus (*Eustoma grandiflorum* 'Echo Pure White') and 'Aretha' (a bi-colour Ecuadorian rose).

THIS PAGE This classic wired bouquet is made entirely of stephanotis, which is beautifully fragrant and always popular. The star-shaped flowers are individually wired and arranged with camellia leaves around the edge. The wires creating the handle are covered in satin ribbon. OPPOSITE A rich and brightly coloured bouquet created for a bride who chose deep purple for her wedding gown. The design is spiralled and tied. It includes the fashionable burgundy rose 'Black Baccara', the pink rose 'Milano' and *Viburnum opulus*. Purple lisianthus adds movement with its lovely tendrils and buds. The pink and yellow gloriosa pull together the pink and acid green. It is edged with glossy green camellia leaves and finished with a purple satin bow.

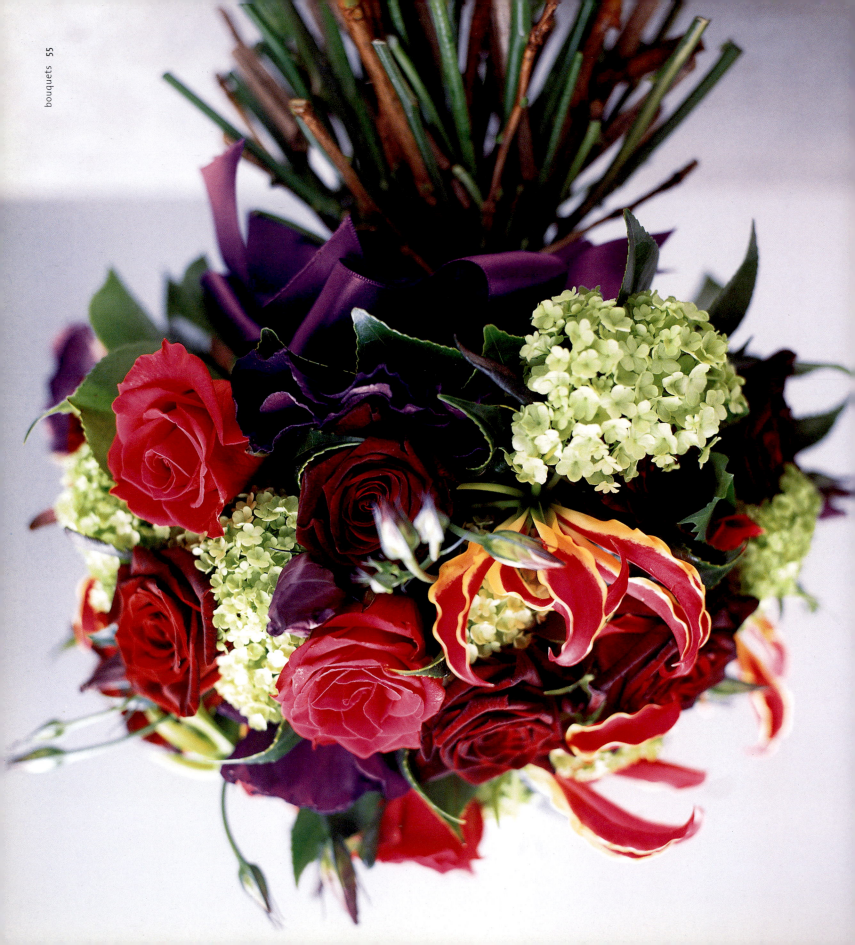

THIS PAGE An autumnal grouped posy including huge ornamental cabbage (*Brassica oleracea* 'Sunrise '99'), balanced against groups of three velvety 'Grand Prix' roses, hydrangea flower heads (*Hydrangea macrophylla* 'Rotshwartz'), rosehips (*Rosa* 'Sensation') and seeded eucalyptus. OPPOSITE An over-arm bouquet of white calla lilies and green 'Midori' anthuriums edged with dark ligularia leaves is tied with white ribbon.

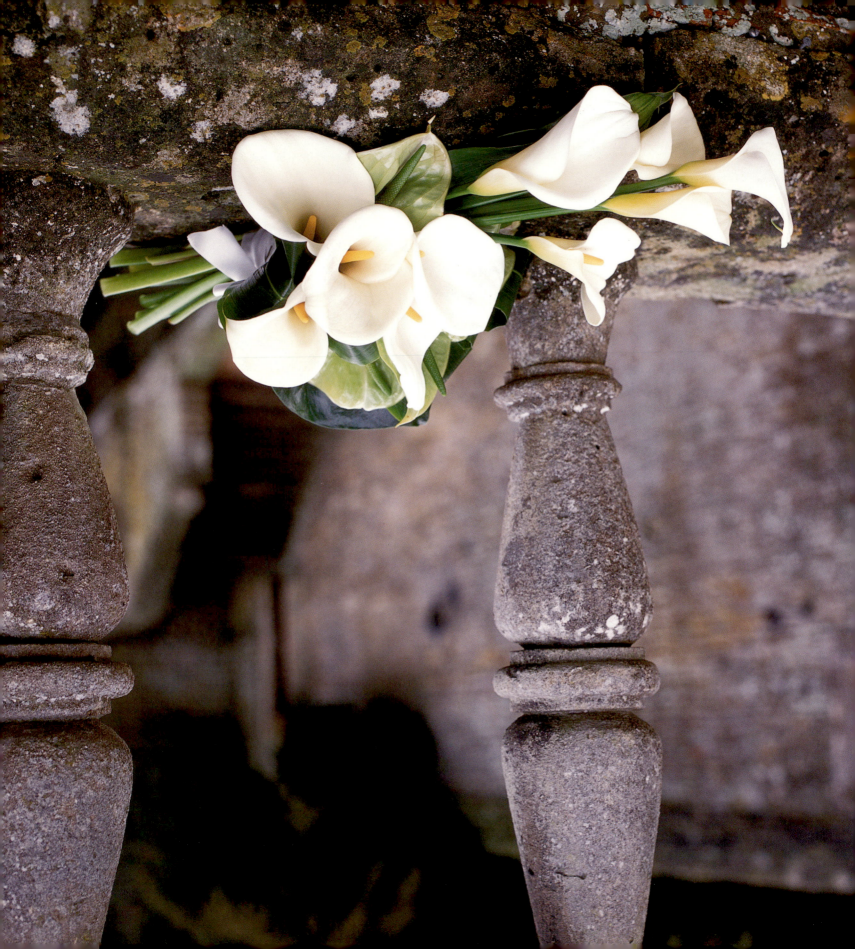

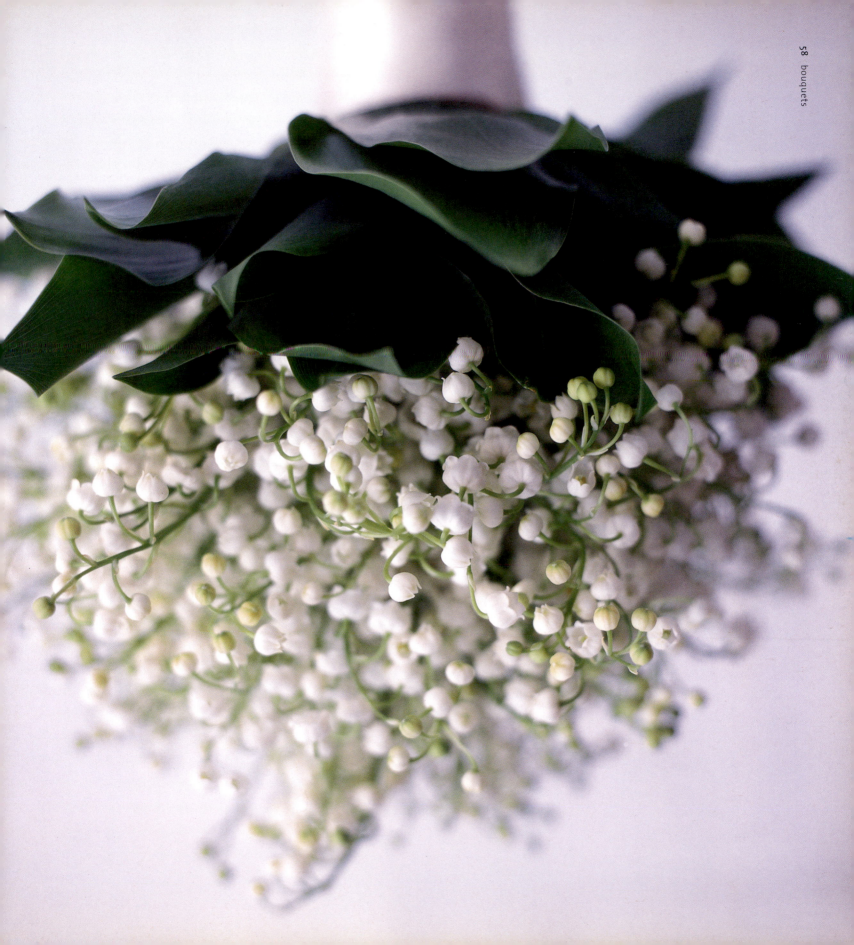

Small delicate flowers as shown on these two pages require a generous number of stems to look effective. **OPPOSITE** A massed lily-of-the-valley bouquet, such as this featuring the pure white species *Convallaria majalis*, requires hundreds of spires of the sweet-scented flower to create an impact. Although lily-of-the-valley is available all the year round grown under glass, it is generally at its best, most plentiful and less expensive at the end of April and beginning of May. **THIS PAGE** Delicate velvety chocolate cosmos (*Cosmos atrosanguineus* 'Black Beauty') are prized for their deep colour and heavenly scent of chocolate – the perfect choice for a chocoholic!

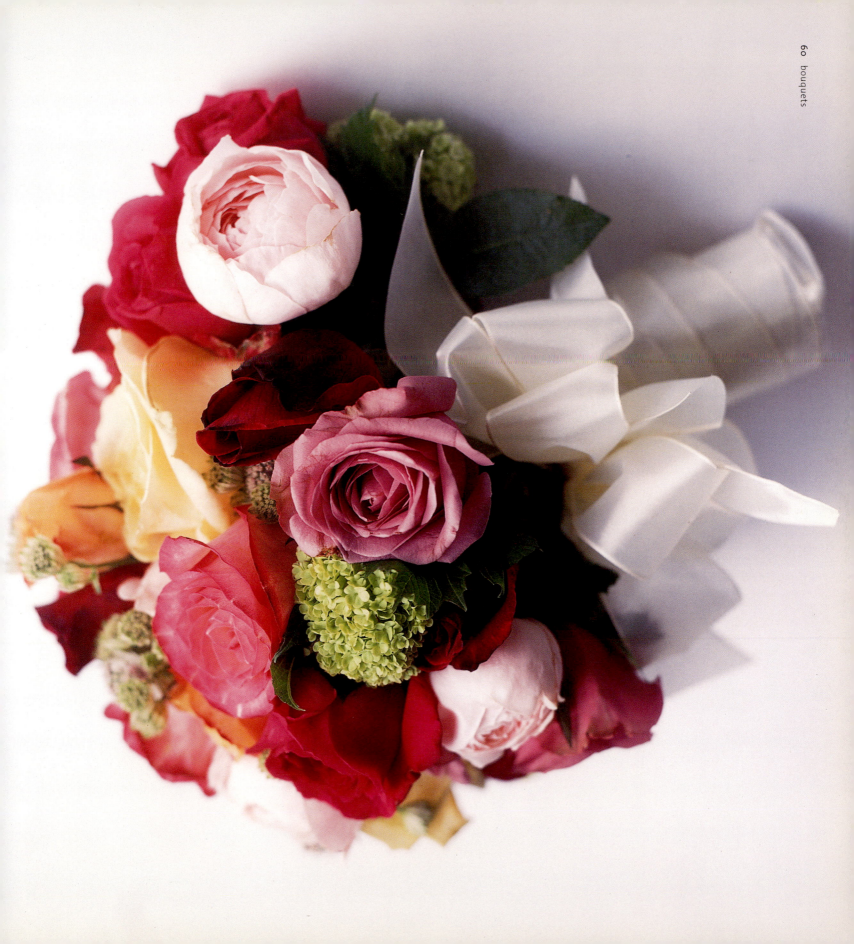

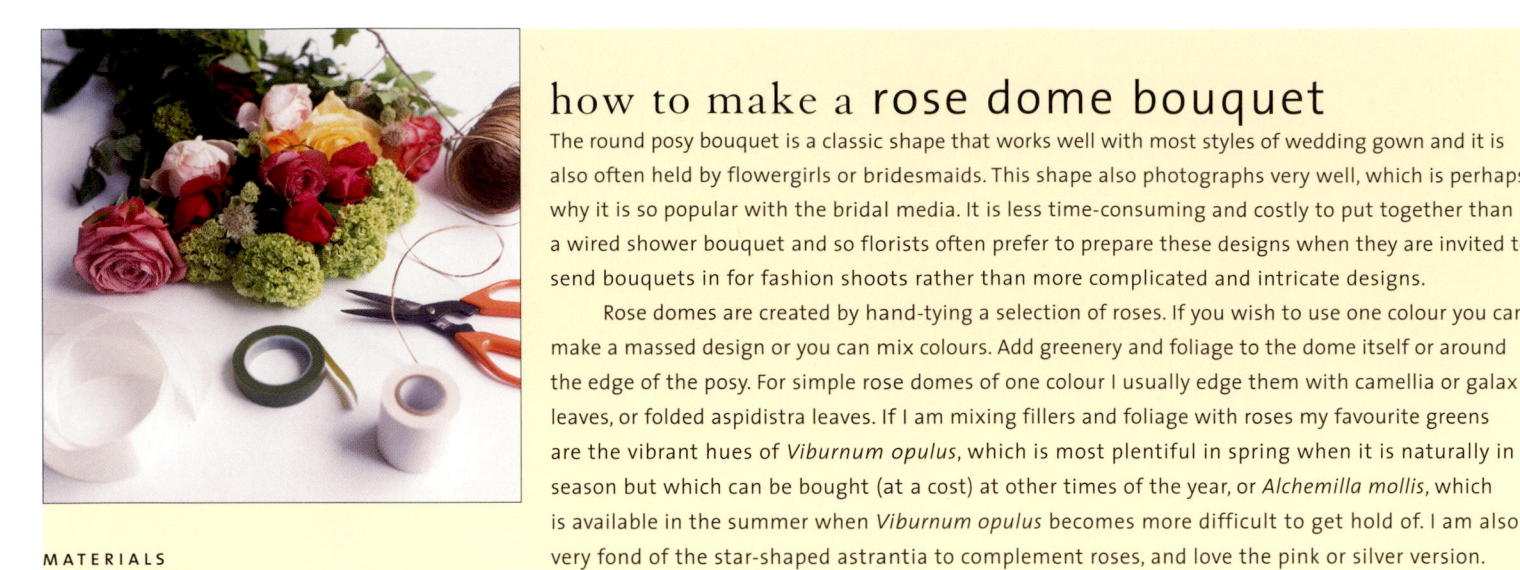

how to make a **rose dome bouquet**

The round posy bouquet is a classic shape that works well with most styles of wedding gown and it is also often held by flowergirls or bridesmaids. This shape also photographs very well, which is perhaps why it is so popular with the bridal media. It is less time-consuming and costly to put together than a wired shower bouquet and so florists often prefer to prepare these designs when they are invited to send bouquets in for fashion shoots rather than more complicated and intricate designs.

Rose domes are created by hand-tying a selection of roses. If you wish to use one colour you can make a massed design or you can mix colours. Add greenery and foliage to the dome itself or around the edge of the posy. For simple rose domes of one colour I usually edge them with camellia or galax leaves, or folded aspidistra leaves. If I am mixing fillers and foliage with roses my favourite greens are the vibrant hues of *Viburnum opulus*, which is most plentiful in spring when it is naturally in season but which can be bought (at a cost) at other times of the year, or *Alchemilla mollis*, which is available in the summer when *Viburnum opulus* becomes more difficult to get hold of. I am also very fond of the star-shaped astrantia to complement roses, and love the pink or silver version.

You can finish a posy by either leaving the stems natural and trimming with a bow around the binding point or by covering the handle with ribbon secured with double-sided tape.

MATERIALS

40 garden roses (mixed colours)
5 stems of *Viburnum opulus*
Reel of double-sided tape
Green gutta-percha tape
String
Ribbon
Scissors
Knife

STEP BY STEP

1 First clean your roses and remove all the lower foliage. Strip the rose stems of thorns. Take a sharp knife and gently prise them off by moving the blade down the length of the stem.
2 Take a central rose and – holding it between your thumb and first finger – add flowers at an angle to the left-hand side. Add about five flowers and then twist the bunch (using your right hand to move it but keeping it in your left hand). Add a further five flowers and twist again.
3 Tie your posy tightly underneath the flower heads so that it is firmly held together and then trim all the stems to the width of your hand. Tie again at the bottom of the stems to form the handle and then, starting from the base of the heads, bind to the tip with the green gutta-percha tape.
4 To hide the stems, run double-sided tape down either side and cover lengthways with two to four strips of ribbon. Add another strip around the handle working from the top to the bottom and then back to the top. Secure with a bow made from three loops and one central ribbon.

how to make a victorian posy

Much of Victorian design is both neat and fussy in its detail and this floral arrangement of concentric circles of flowers is known as a Victorian posy in the flower world. The use of a number of different flowers in a rigid design was often highly symbolic and designed to convey a specific meaning. (Very little of this 'floral language' is used today in our choice of flowers and plants but much of the symbolism remains.) It was during this time that the floristry profession started to emerge. Very often these 'florists' were gardeners attached to large estates and gardens, who learnt to wire individual heads from flowers to create more complicated and intricate designs. Wiring flowers allows you to have much more control over them and so the idea of creating a wired concentric-circle posy became very fashionable. In keeping with much of nineteenth-century design these posies were quite fussy and would include a number of smaller flowers wired and then placed in circles around a larger central flower. Wiring is very time consuming and it also means that you have to work very close to the deadline of the event because the flowers are removed from the stem and are no longer able to drink water.

Here I have shown how to make a Victorian posy without any wire and the key to success is choosing the right flowers to create this design. Small-headed flowers such as violets, forget-me-nots, muscari, narcissus, pinks, sweet peas and roses are very suitable.

MATERIALS

10 bunches of grape hyacinths (muscari)
3 bunches of sweet peas
12 'Vendela' roses
2 bunches of forget-me-nots
1 central rose
Scissors
Strong tape
Ribbon

STEP BY STEP

1 First clean all the foliage and thorns from the roses and clean the forget-me nots. Carefully arrange the forget-me-nots around the central rose in your left hand. Keep turning the bunch with your right hand as you are doing this to enable you to make a neat circle of the blue flowers around the central single rose.

2 Next add the 'Vendela' roses just a little lower than the height of the forget-me-nots – creating the lovely domed shape. Make sure that you are placing the roses at exactly the same height all around to create a defined circular shape.

3 Next, you are ready to add the delicate sweet peas. Keep your left hand very relaxed as you add them and then use your right hand to move the bunch so that you are working on all sides.

4 Finally add bunches of five grape hyacinths at a time, placing them lower than the sweet peas – continue working on all sides of the bunch. Work round three times in all (adding three layers of the grape hyacinths) so that you have a sumptuously bunched finshed effect.

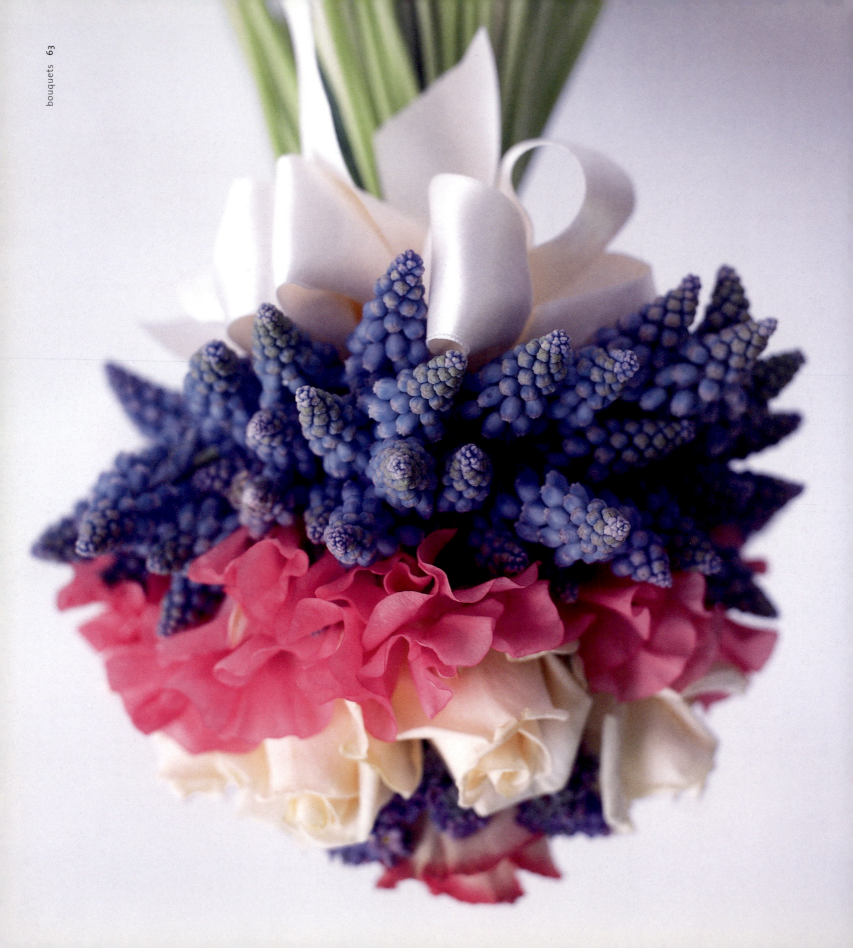

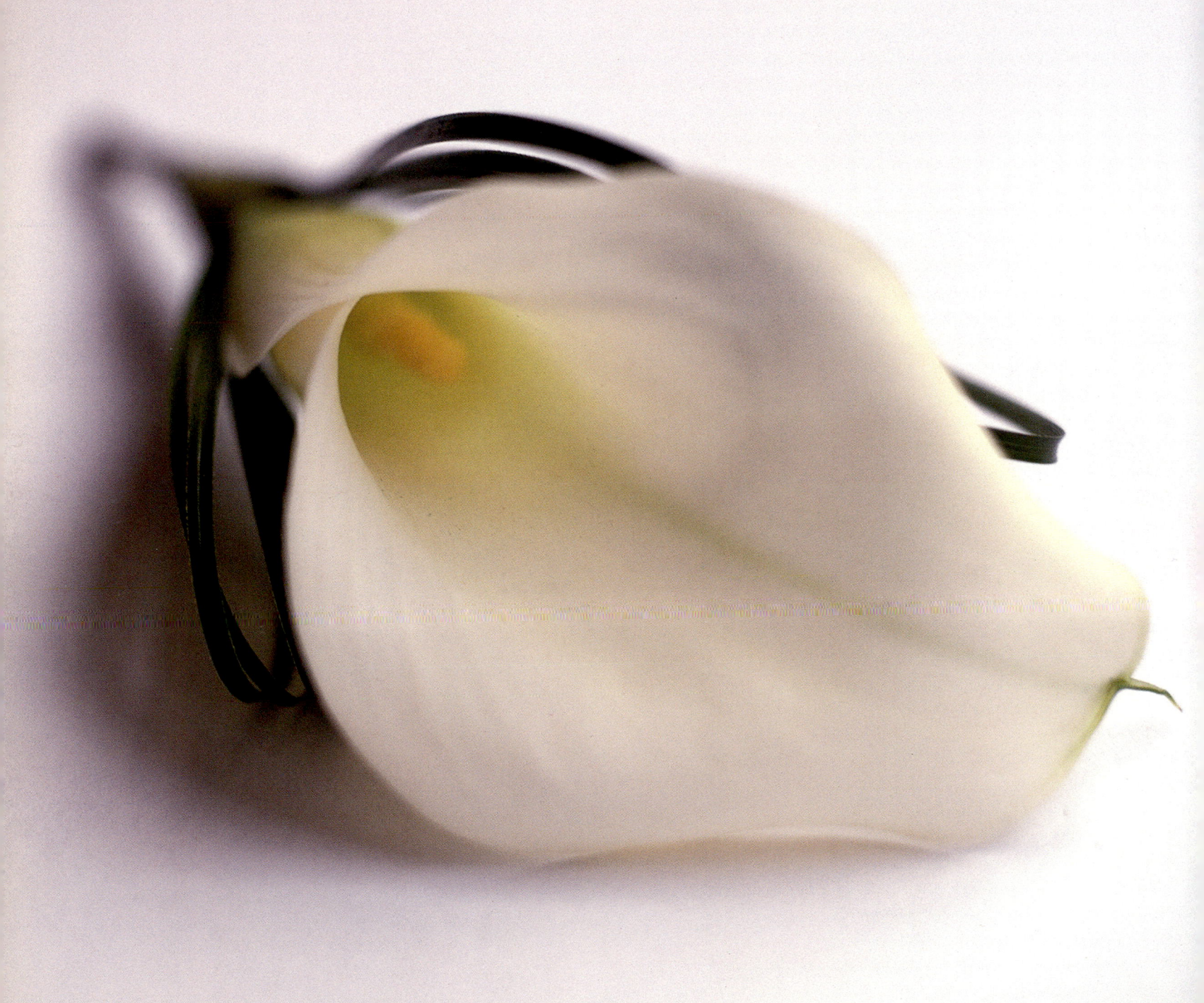

floral accessories buttonholes **corsages** details

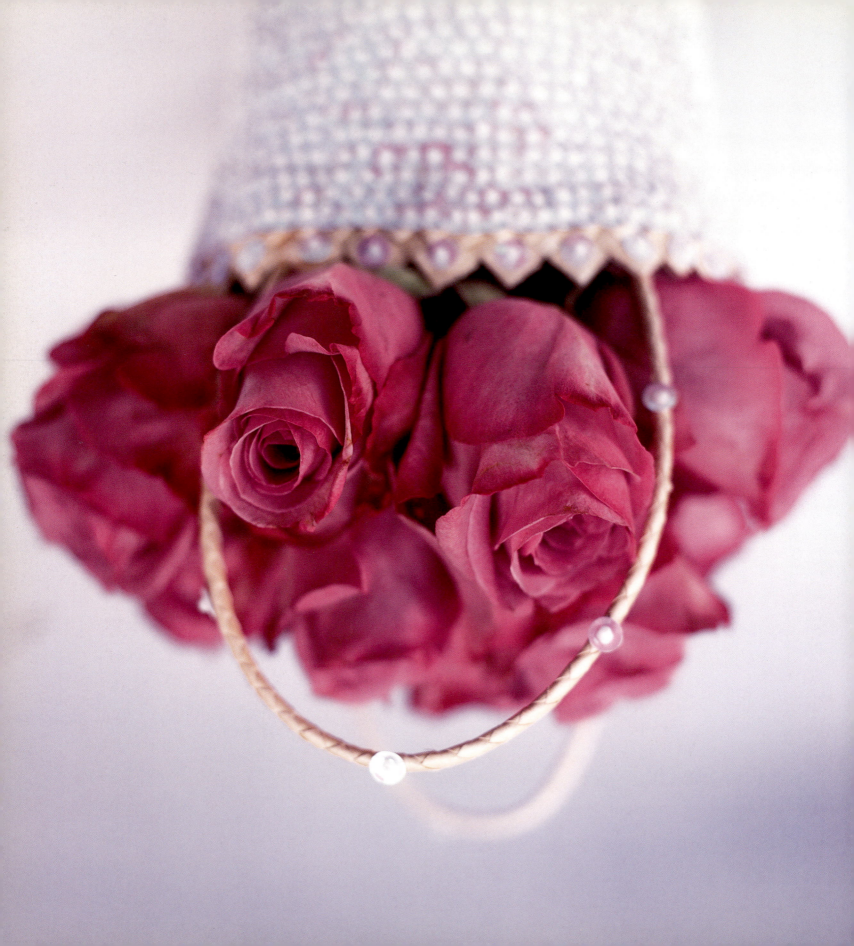

creating a theme

In addition to her own bouquet, a bride may plan many other floral accessories, both for herself and for certain key members of the wedding party. The outfits for the groomsmen, ushers, bridesmaids, flower girls, ring-bearers, pages and, of course, the immediate family all go toward creating the total look for her wedding day. Their clothes need to tone with the bride's dress and complement the overall theme of the wedding and this is equally true of any floral accessories they wear. They are intended to enhance but not outshine the bride!

flowers in the hair

Flowers worn by the bride in her hair on her wedding day may be one of the most exquisite accessories. Wearing a ring of flowers is a tradition that dates from Ancient Greece. Queen Victoria helped to revive this classic trend when she was married wearing a crown of orange blossom, and in more recent times that epitome of style, the Hollywood actress Audrey Hepburn, wore a simple ring of rose buds on her head for her wedding in 1954. This is the most popular floral accessory, and it should be planned in conjunction with your bouquet and will involve a collaboration between your hairdresser and your florist. Your choice of headdress will also be influenced by how you decide to wear your hair and whether or not you are going to wear a veil.

Brides can choose to wear a single large flower, a number of small wired florets (individual rose buds or stephanotis, for example), a full Alice band, a floral circlet or a tiara, which is usually made from very delicate florets of flowers (such as hyacinths, stephanotis or tuberose pips). An Alice band or a comb of flowers is most often worn in front of the veil and this is a clever technique for adding a little more to your height. In recent years jewelled tiaras have become more popular with brides for creating this effect but many people still opt for a fresh floral headdress to complement their bouquet.

Fresh flowers near your face can make you look younger, your skin rosier and your eyes brighter. It is, after all, probably the only time you are going to be able to wear flowers in your hair and there is something wonderfully indulgent about bedecking yourself with fresh flowers. However, if you are planning a headdress then it is important that you have a run through with your hairdresser and it is certainly worth asking your florist to make a trial headdress for you as you do not want any snags or surprises on the day!

Some brides may choose to wear a hat and this can also be decorated with fresh flowers and foliage. Ideally flowers are suited to a wider brimmed hat. Midsummer brides or more informal brides may choose this option and it is also often a popular choice for the more mature or second-time bride. Your florist will wire up the flowers and attach them to your hat and deliver the two together on your wedding day. Sometimes the mother of the bride or groom may choose this accessory instead of wearing a corsage. Matrons-of-honour may also prefer this and some of your guests will like the idea too.

necklaces and bracelets

It is customary in India to wear floral leis around the neck or wrist and we often make these for weddings involving a mix of cultures. At a Hindu wedding the bride and groom exchange sumptuous garlands, mainly of red and white flowers decorated with silver and assembled by threading the flower head onto a wire. Carnations work well for these as they are relatively inexpensive (a factor when so many flower heads are needed) and are durable.

Some brides like to break with convention and wear something more unusual, such as a floral boa or a necklace of flowers. If you do choose a necklace you need to

have a good elegant neck so do experiment first! Wrist corsages can also add glamour to a bridal dress and look fabulous on more mature bridesmaids or matrons-of-honour. Some brides choose to have their shoes adorned with flowers that peep out under the gown as they walk. If you are planning something out of the ordinary it is worth spending a little bit more money and asking your florist to make you a prototype to try out. That way you can be sure you are happy with your ideas. If you wish to sew flower heads onto your dress, you will have to ask your florist to wire them so that the stem is removed making it easier for you to attach them to your gown. A few miniature rose heads sewn on to the veil can look very romantic.

Flowers aren't just for the bride! For one midsummer wedding in Italy I made a wild floral headdress for the groom as well as the bride. For another groom I made a floral adornment to wear as a scarf and even – for another incurable romantic – a Cupid's bow and arrow! The scope and nature of the floral accessories you can have at your wedding is limited only by your imagination and personal preference and the skill and creativity of the designer you are working with.

accessories for the young

Younger bridesmaids, flower girls, pageboys and young ring-bearers are often dressed more seasonally with more attention to the time of year than the bride. In winter bridesmaids may wear

OPPOSITE Individually wiring flower heads and having your hairdresser pin them into your hair is a pretty way of using flowers as an accessory for adult bridesmaids or matrons-of-honour. The scented, star-shaped pips of stephanotis are perfect for this because they are quite waxy and long lasting. **ABOVE, LEFT TO RIGHT** Classic willow bridesmaid's basket filled with white rose-buds, sweet peas and stephanotis; Little sequinned bags filled with roses make an alternative to a basket. Again these type of floral accessories are perfect for a younger bridesmaid to carry as they can be put down.

fake fur muffs decorated with flowers and page boys may be dressed in rich tartan or velvet. How you decide to dress your attendants will largely depend on their ages, the time of the year and any theme you are planning for your wedding. Your contemporaries are not going to speak to you again if you dress them in a sugar-almond pink tutu and give them a set of iridescent wings and a floral wand, but your three-year-old niece will undoubtedly think it the highlight of the year! Floral headdresses are best for the youngest bridesmaids and there are two types that are suitable for young children with especially fine hair – a circlet that goes all round the head and sits on the crown or an Alice band, where the flowers are wired onto a frame. It is a good idea to give your florist a dimension for the circlet as a guide. How long it is will

depend on how the bridesmaid is going to wear it; however they are usually fastened with a hook, which can be adjusted on the day.

Sometimes an Alice band can be the most practical option as you can ask your bridesmaid to break one in before having your florist attach the flowers and deliver it on the day. You may even ask your dressmaker to cover a band with fabric to match the bridesmaids' dresses. Some bridesmaids are more stoical than others about wearing headdresses and it is worth spending a little time thinking about this to avoid a floral headdress causing a high drama just before your big moment. If you are lucky enough to have your hairdresser with you while you are dressing then ask them to fit the floral headdresses for your attendants.

There is no limit to the floral accessories you can add to your wedding for your young attendants. For a festive wedding in winter I have created miniature Christmas trees and kissing balls fashioned from woven mistletoe for the bridesmaids to carry. At one late afternoon wedding in the autumn the older pages carried storm lanterns and for another eight bridesmaids carried candles on brass trays decorated with ivies, which seemed quite adventurous but passed without incident! We have made hoops of hips and berries in the autumn and trugs of country wheat and harvested fruits for a wedding in late September.

I have seen small bridesmaids dressed as fairies or miniature pre-Raphaelite beauties. To make your bridesmaids look like little Greek goddesses use long ruscus leaves and stephanotis pips to make a simple green-and-white headdress. One of my favourite accessories for a small bridesmaid is the flower ball or pomander. These can be created from moss or floral foam and look very cute. They also work well if the bride has chosen a dome of roses as they match. Ask your florist to wire and sew some flowers on your bridesmaids' shoes; this works particularly well with ballet shoes or satin slippers.

Page boys do not usually carry anything although they often sport a miniature rosebud and their costumes vary from the traditional and formal to military-inspired with sailor suits still being a classic. Pages may be asked to carry a prayer book or a basket of petals to throw after the ceremony. Flowers are wired and attached to the book as a marker. Traditionally they were

THIS PAGE Here a hand-held storm lantern is decorated with ivy and three open 'Queensday' roses. Other unusual accessories include floral wands for 'fairies', teddy bears, moss cushions for ring-bearers, sprays for prayer books, leis and flower boas, a shepherdess's crook and a Cupid's bow and arrow for a ring-bearer.

made from white flowers, either a mixture of roses and orchids or a single type of flower, such as the beautiful, and appropriately named, Easter lily. Ring bearers often have a cushion made from moss or flower heads to take to the altar.

baskets of flowers
Baskets filled with cut flowers are the most popular bridesmaid's accessory. One of the main advantages of a basket is that it allows the bridesmaid to put down her flowers when necessary while a bouquet if constantly handled can become damaged around the edges and start to droop. Baskets of petals are also very popular and attendants can sprinkle petals on the floor before the entrance of the bride to create a gorgeous scent. Alternatively, rose petals can be put into pretty paper cones and handed out to all the guests to scatter at the end of the ceremony.

choosing flowers for your attendants
When choosing flowers for your attendants to carry remember that they should complement your overall scheme and be appropriate to your attendants' outfits and size, as you do not want to overburden them. An experienced florist will advise you on

this. Most often bridesmaids carry smaller posies, as this is the least expensive option. The flowers are usually a little more colourful than the bridal bouquet and are made in proportion to the size of the person carrying them so be sure to let your designer know their ages. Make sure that your chief bridesmaid shows the smaller attendants how to hold their flowers and to keep their arms relaxed so that they look their best as they walk into the ceremony.

buttonholes As well as the other wedding

flowers it is customary to order special buttonholes for your fiancé, his father and grandfather and your father, the best man and all the ushers. These buttonholes usually chosen to suit the men's ties and the other flowers, so white is often the safest and easiest option, perhaps picking a special colour for your own father and fiancé . Although it is a lovely idea to want to give all your guests a floral accessory such as a buttonhole it is quite expensive and can be needlessly extravagant. In my experience very often people do not want to pin a flower onto their outfit, so these gifts are passed by. If you are going to make this gesture, make sure you appoint a particular usher to offer the buttonholes to each guest as they arrive at the ceremony and make sure your florist has labelled any special flowers so that they can be offered to the appropriate person.

decorating bags It is traditional for mothers and grandmothers of the happy cou-

ple to have larger buttonholes or corsages to wear. These are usually chosen to suit their outfits and may be pinned onto handbags to protect their clothes. If you want a florist to do this for you it is essential to check that the bag is suitable, it works best if the bag is rigid rather than a soft fabric. Leave it

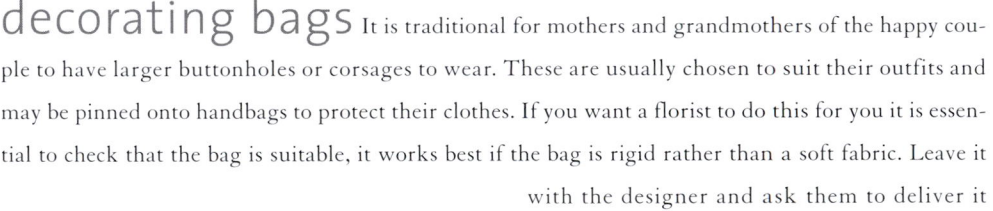

with the designer and ask them to deliver it

decorated on the day. For a handbag corsage I love to use gardenias or roses, which can be wired onto the strap or across the front if it is clutch style. Single orchids or smaller sprays of blooms (often known collectively as Singapore orchids) are perfect for corsages as they are very durable and long lasting and come in a huge range of colours. For a sweetly scented corsage, you can choose freesias, stephanotis, garden roses or gardenia. If a bag corsage isn't appropriate a flower to trim a hat is a good alternative to wearing a corsage or but-tonhole. A flower wired into the hair is another possibility and for sleeveless dresses a wrist corsage is also an option to consider.

You can adorn all parents, grandparents, siblings and special guests with flowers as a symbol of unity with your new family and as a way of letting all the rest of the guests know who is special!

pretty in pink

an impressive venue can really set the tone of a wedding. When Jenny and Tim decided to marry they were one of a select few couples who are lucky enough to enjoy the honour of holding their ceremony in the crypt of St Paul's Cathedral, as Tim's father has been awarded a CBE.

On one of her earliest visits to my shop Jenny picked out a deep pink calla lily for her own bouquet, which inspired the overall cream and pink floral theme. This was carried through to the other wedding flowers, which included the creamy 'Vendela' rose and 'Laminuette', which is a cream rose edged with pink. Jenny then spent a long time tracking down the fabric for her bridesmaids' dresses to match her bridal flowers. She finally found soft, dusky-pink shot silk. For herself, she decided to have a simple hand-tied shower of the long-stemmed calla lilies she had originally chosen to carry on the day. To co-ordinate with Jenny, Tim wore a 'Black Baccara' rose buttonhole, while each of the groomsmen wore 'Vendela' roses.

For the chapel we decorated round ligustrum trees with roses and then positioned two large pedestals and decorations at the ends of the pews. Following the ceremony, the bridal party were taken to a naval and military club for a drinks party with 200 guests, canapés, the speeches and the champagne toast as well as the cutting of the cake. They then settled down for the wedding breakfast with a more intimate group of family, as the venue had limited space for dinner. For this richly coloured room, Jenny chose to have lots of candlelight, so to make an impression on half the tables we used tall copper candelabras, each holding eight candlelights. On the other half of the tables we had low arrangements of glass cubes that were themselves surrounded by candlelights and then filled with equisetum topped with sweet peas, roses and lisianthus.

ABOVE Jenny and Tim steal a kiss after the ceremony. Tim's tie and buttonhole match Jenny's beautiful shower bouquet of pink calla lilies perfectly, while his green waistcoat tones with the rich green foliage used throughout for the floral accessories.

The flowers had to be removed from St Paul's immediately after the ceremony so we were able to re-use them at the reception venue. While the guests were enjoying their drinks and canapés we brought the flowers in through the back door and garlanded the stairs with the flowers that had been used to decorate the pew ends at the church. Many more of Jenny and Tim's friends returned after the family dinner and even more joined them to dance the night away in a marquee that had been erected in an adjoining courtyard.

CLOCKWISE FROM ABOVE The bridal party leave the ceremony, Jenny holding her shower bouquet of calla lilies and the bridesmaids wearing circlets of roses and sweet peas; An apprehensive bridesmaid tries out her floral headdress. It's a good idea to ask your bridesmaid to break in a headdress before decorating it for the ceremony; Jenny and Tim smiling at their guests as they leave the chapel. Jenny's beautiful shower bouquet suits a formal setting such as this, and looks perfect with her classic gown and long veil; Tim's groomsmen line up on the steps of the church, sporting their 'Vendela' rose buttonholes. Tailored jackets such as these often have a small loop behind the lapel to anchor the buttonhole.

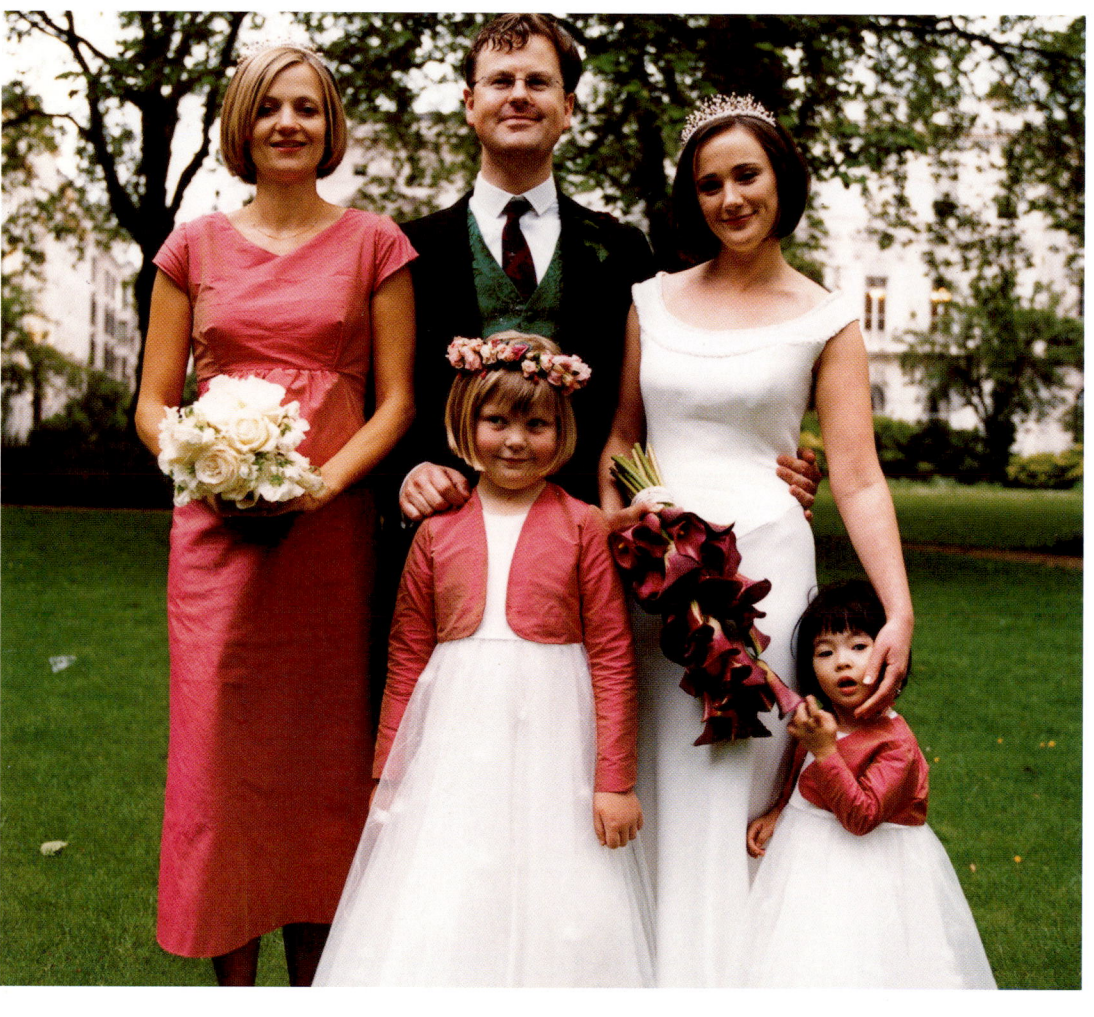

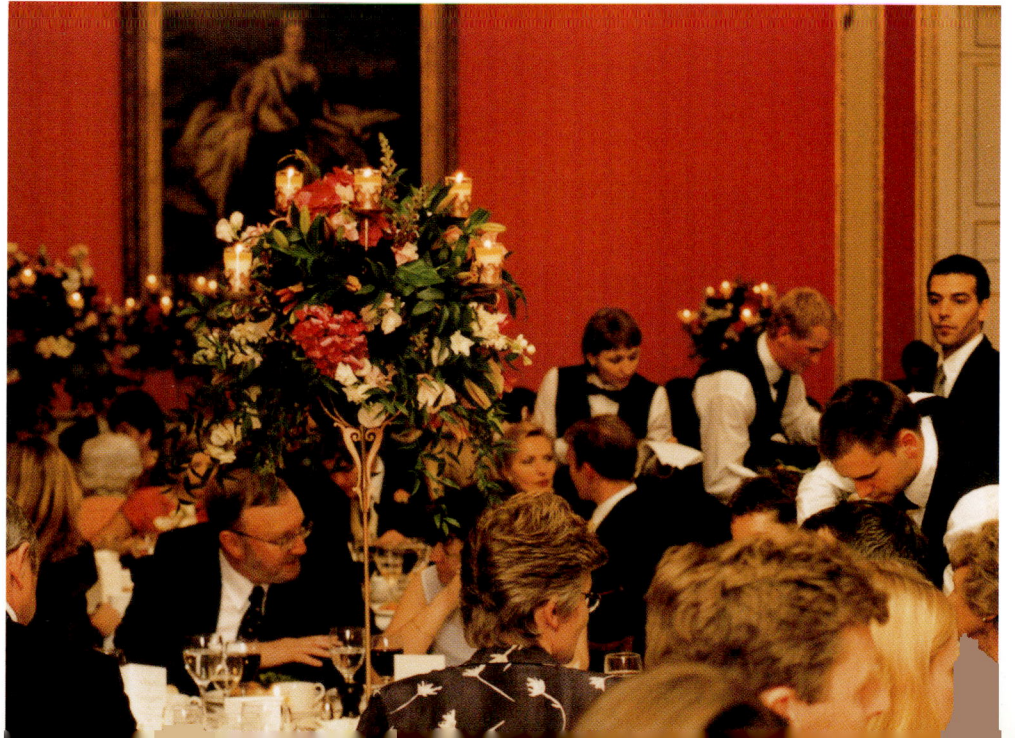

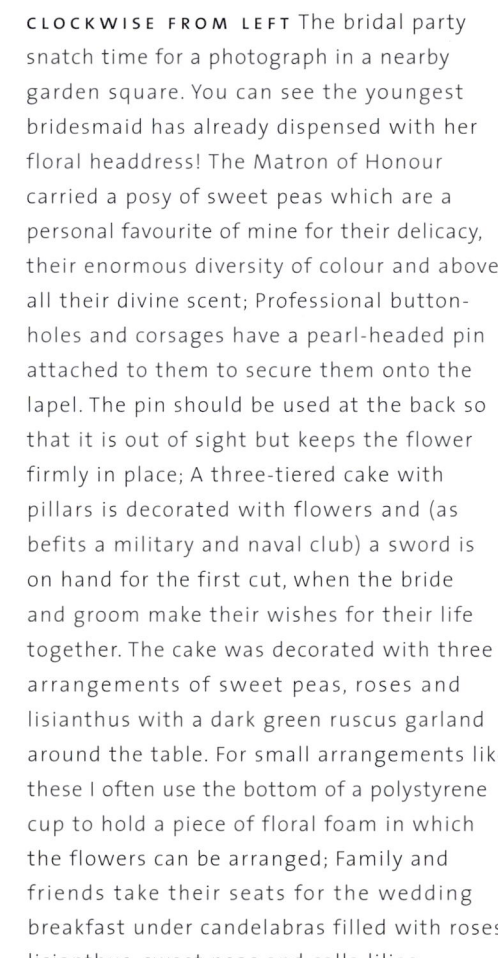

> "Paula's flowers were an inspiration and she made sure that every detail was perfect on the day." JENNY

CLOCKWISE FROM LEFT The bridal party snatch time for a photograph in a nearby garden square. You can see the youngest bridesmaid has already dispensed with her floral headdress! The Matron of Honour carried a posy of sweet peas which are a personal favourite of mine for their delicacy, their enormous diversity of colour and above all their divine scent; Professional button-holes and corsages have a pearl-headed pin attached to them to secure them onto the lapel. The pin should be used at the back so that it is out of sight but keeps the flower firmly in place; A three-tiered cake with pillars is decorated with flowers and (as befits a military and naval club) a sword is on hand for the first cut, when the bride and groom make their wishes for their life together. The cake was decorated with three arrangements of sweet peas, roses and lisianthus with a dark green ruscus garland around the table. For small arrangements like these I often use the bottom of a polystyrene cup to hold a piece of floral foam in which the flowers can be arranged; Family and friends take their seats for the wedding breakfast under candelabras filled with roses, lisianthus, sweet peas and calla lilies.

buttonholes

thistle with berries A late summer buttonhole of two rudbeckia seedheads (*Rudbeckia hirta*) with montbretia berries (*Crocosmia* 'Lucifer') and backed with three cotinus leaves (*Cotinus coggygria* 'Royal Purple').

red & pink A simple rose buttonhole (*Rosa* 'Jacaranda') can be made more seasonal and exotic by adding a celosia head (*Celosia* var. *cristata* 'No. 9') brown alder berries (*Alnus*) and black *Viburnum tinus* berries.

spiky bloom Round-shaped flowers such as this medium-sized single dahlia (*Dahlia* 'Bishop of Llandaff') make perfect buttonholes. Other good round shapes include smaller gerberas known as 'Germini', miniature sunflowers (*Helianthus annuus*), ranunculus, and daisies such as *Leucanthemum vulgare*.

calla & berries This ever-popular mix of deep pink calla lilies (*Zantedeschia aethiopica* 'Majestic Red') and hypericum berries is often chosen to match the bridal bouquet. Calla lilies have a beautiful flower shape and come in a wide range of colours from deep burgundy, pink, lilac, yellow, and mango through to white.

chillies In autumn there are a number of seedheads, berries and ornamental vegetables that can be wired to make a buttonhole or corsage. Here two sprigs of rosehips (*Rosa* 'Sensation') have been wired with two sprigs of vibrant *Capsicum annuum* and edged with wired dark leaves from the smokebush plant (*Cotinus coggygria* 'Royal Purple').

Buttonholes or corsages are traditionally given to the immediate family, the groomsmen and ushers. (Corsages are larger than buttonholes and are generally constructed using more than one variety of flowers or a group of two or three together with some leaves as backing.) Some couples also like to give each of their guests a flower as a symbol of their love and friendship – small, light flowers are best for this.

THIS PAGE By far the most popular choice of buttonhole is the white rose – here *Rosa* 'Bianca' is shown embellished with a few *Eryngium planum* 'Blue Candle' thistles and dark green ivy. Other popular roses include the pure white 'Akito', champagne 'Vendella', dark burgundy 'Black Baccara', bright red 'Grand Prix', lilac 'Cool Water', fuchsia pink 'Milano' or bright pink 'Barbie', lime green 'Emerald', yellow 'Taxi' and orange 'Milva'.

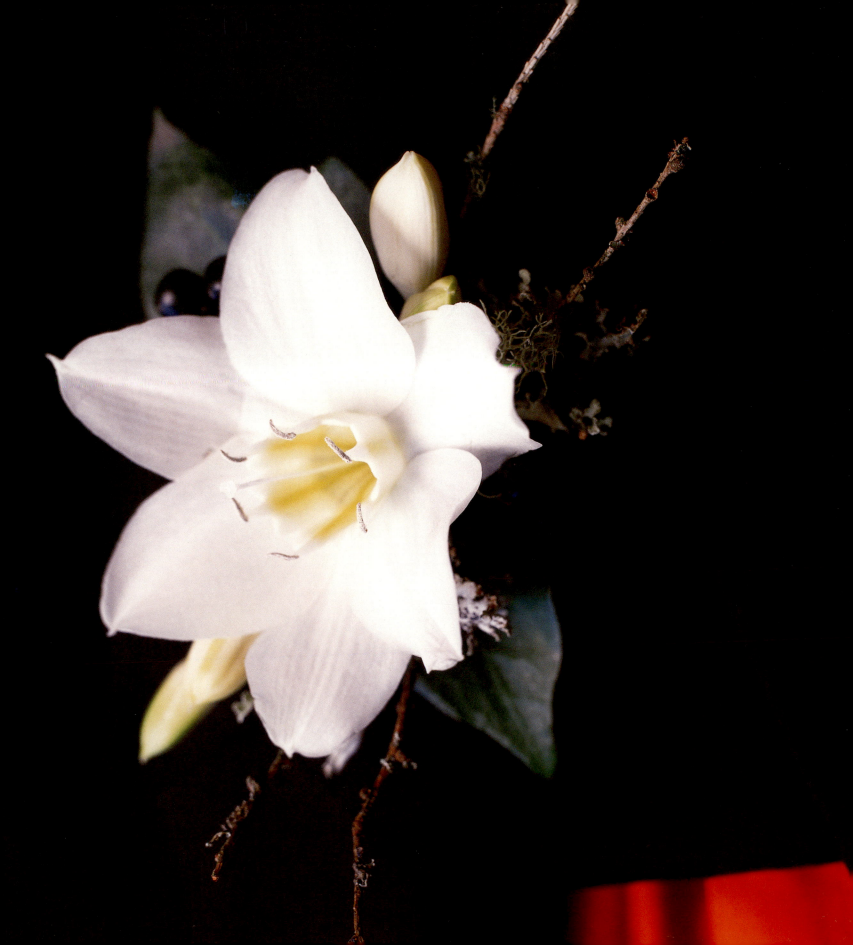

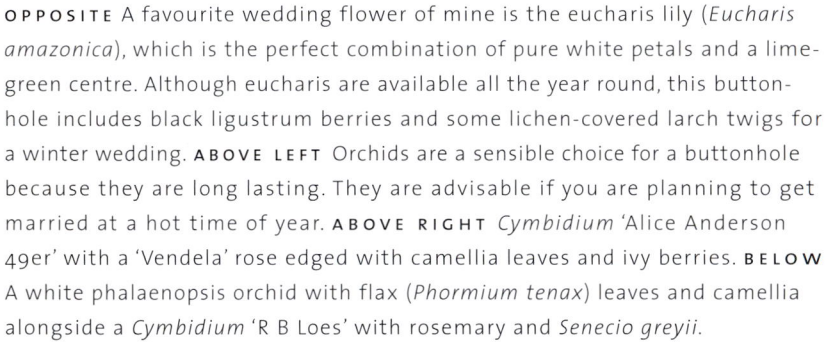

OPPOSITE A favourite wedding flower of mine is the eucharis lily (*Eucharis amazonica*), which is the perfect combination of pure white petals and a lime-green centre. Although eucharis are available all the year round, this button-hole includes black ligustrum berries and some lichen-covered larch twigs for a winter wedding. ABOVE LEFT Orchids are a sensible choice for a buttonhole because they are long lasting. They are advisable if you are planning to get married at a hot time of year. ABOVE RIGHT *Cymbidium* 'Alice Anderson 49er' with a 'Vendela' rose edged with camellia leaves and ivy berries. BELOW A white phalaenopsis orchid with flax (*Phormium tenax*) leaves and camellia alongside a *Cymbidium* 'R B Loes' with rosemary and *Senecio greyii*.

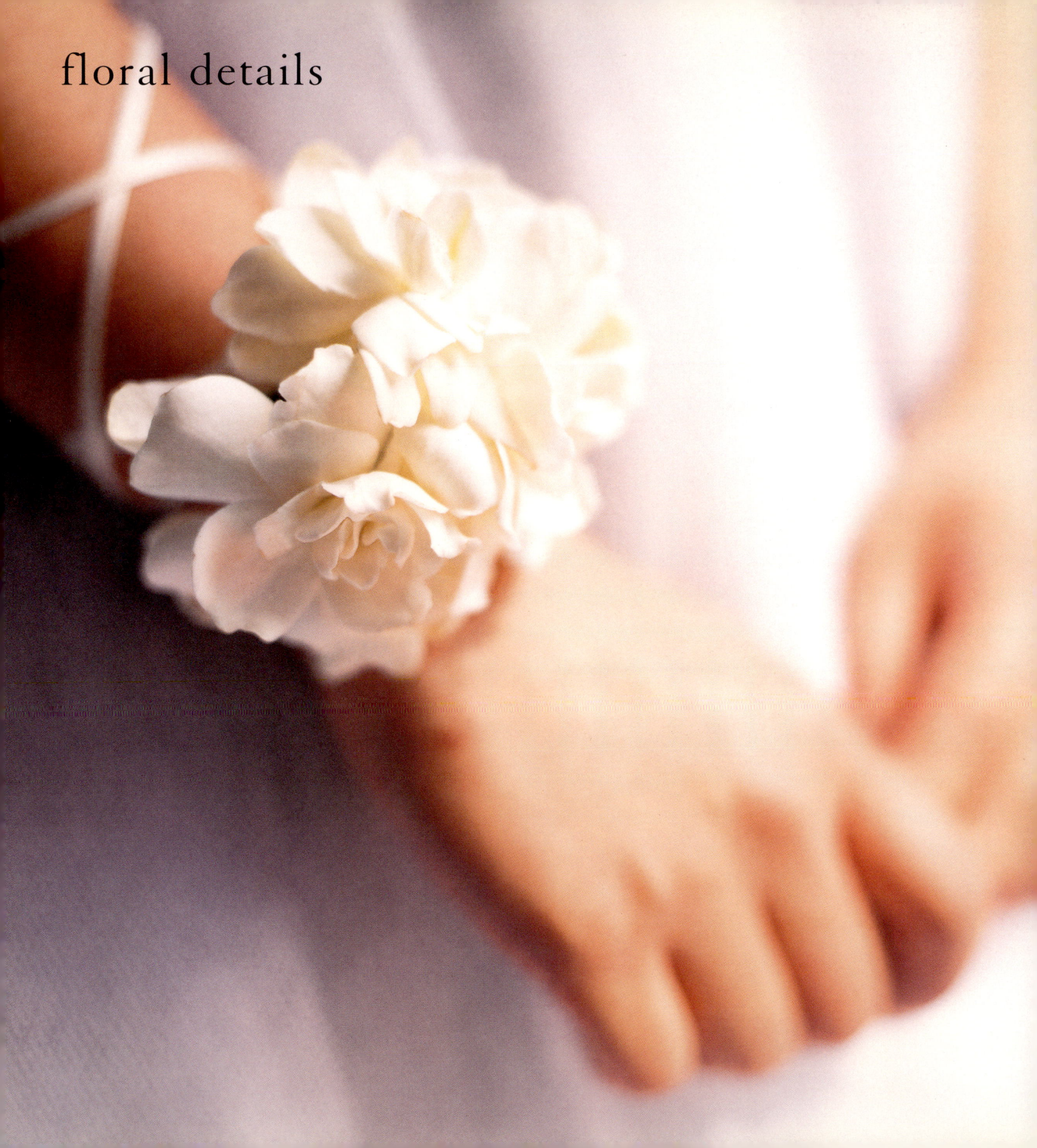

OPPOSITE A wrist corsage is an alternative way of accessorising a bridesmaid or flower girl and is particularly suitable for the very young (or the very mature!) bridesmaid who might not feel comfortable holding a posy. Currently wristlets like these scented gardenias are becoming increasingly popular. ABOVE Wired rosebuds have been sewn onto a pair of ballet slippers to decorate a flower girl. If you wish to pin flowers on to your shoes or outfit, it is advisable to ask the florist to wire the blooms to make it easier to attach them. RIGHT Alice bands are easier to wear than full circlets and here small 'Tamango' rosebuds have been wired and taped with dark green ivy leaves onto a plastic Alice band.

A talented florist will be able to make you any kind of floral accessory you require from Cupid's bow and arrow to a halo for a cherubic bridesmaid. In the past we have been asked to accessorise shoes, bridal gowns, hand bags, hats and even winter muffs. Your florist could create you a pillow of flowers for your ring bearers, fashion a lucky horseshoe from white heather, sculpt a moss teddy bear for young bridesmaids or design a floral crown to complete your veil. By the careful use of wired flower heads many clever and intricate designs can be created to make your wedding truly individual.

ABOVE LEFT Round hoops or wreaths of flowers are an alternative way for your bridesmaids to carry flowers. Hydrangeas, peonies, arum lilies, roses, sweet peas and eucharis lily heads have been wired and taped onto a round metal frame. **ABOVE RIGHT** Singapore orchids (*Dendrobium*) have been individually wired and woven into a bridesmaid's hair. **RIGHT** Decorated prayer books were very fashionable for brides in the fifties and sixties and this is still a pretty way of accessorising books used for readings. Here hellebores, quince (*Chaenomeles japonica*) and spray roses have been wired together and tied to the book with raffia. **OPPOSITE** Offering a corsage or a buttonhole is a lovely way to welcome guests. Here the rare and unusual vanda orchid has been wired into a vibrant corsage. Orchids are my favourite flower for a corsage because they are long lasting and will still look good when the festivities are over.

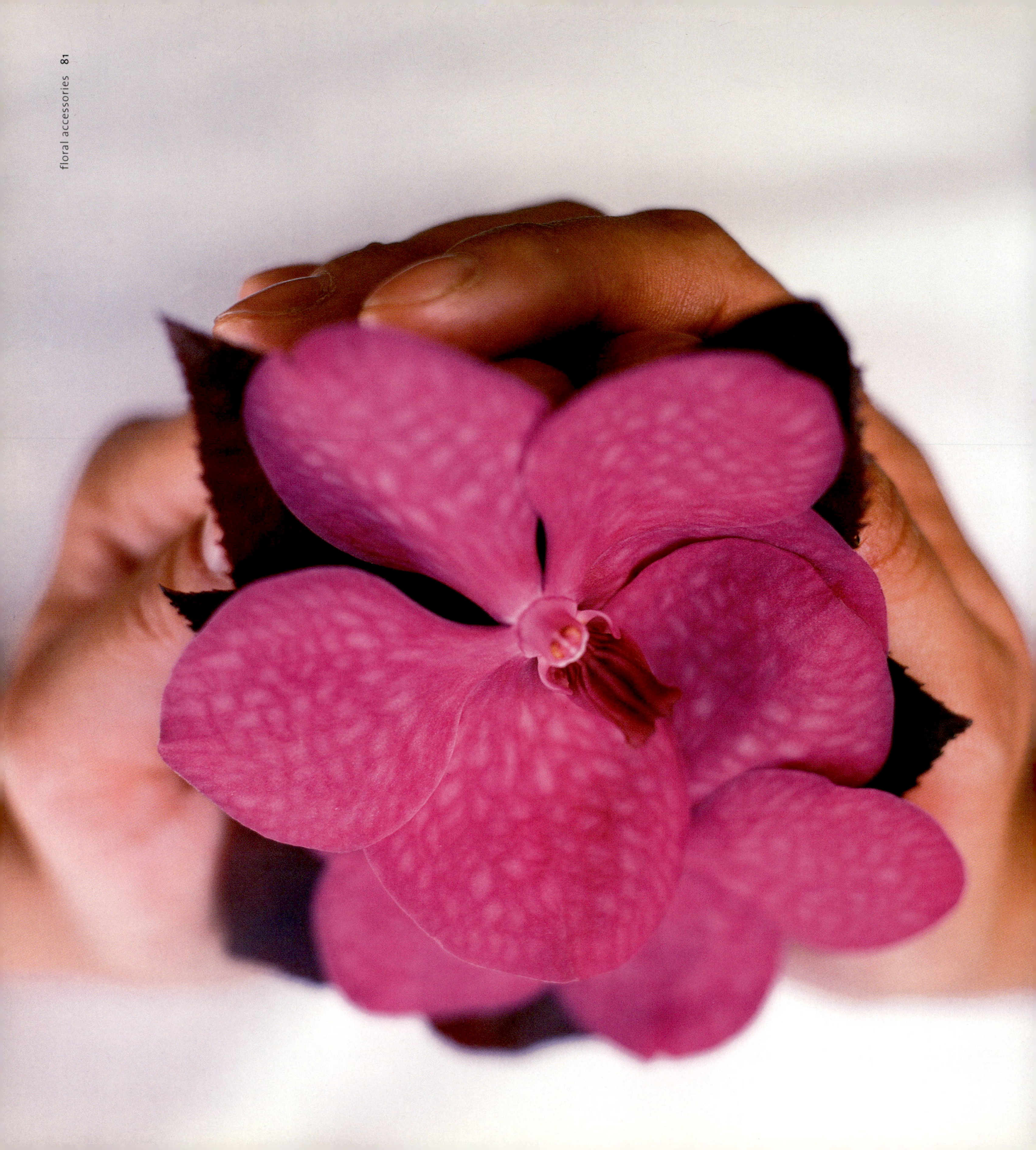

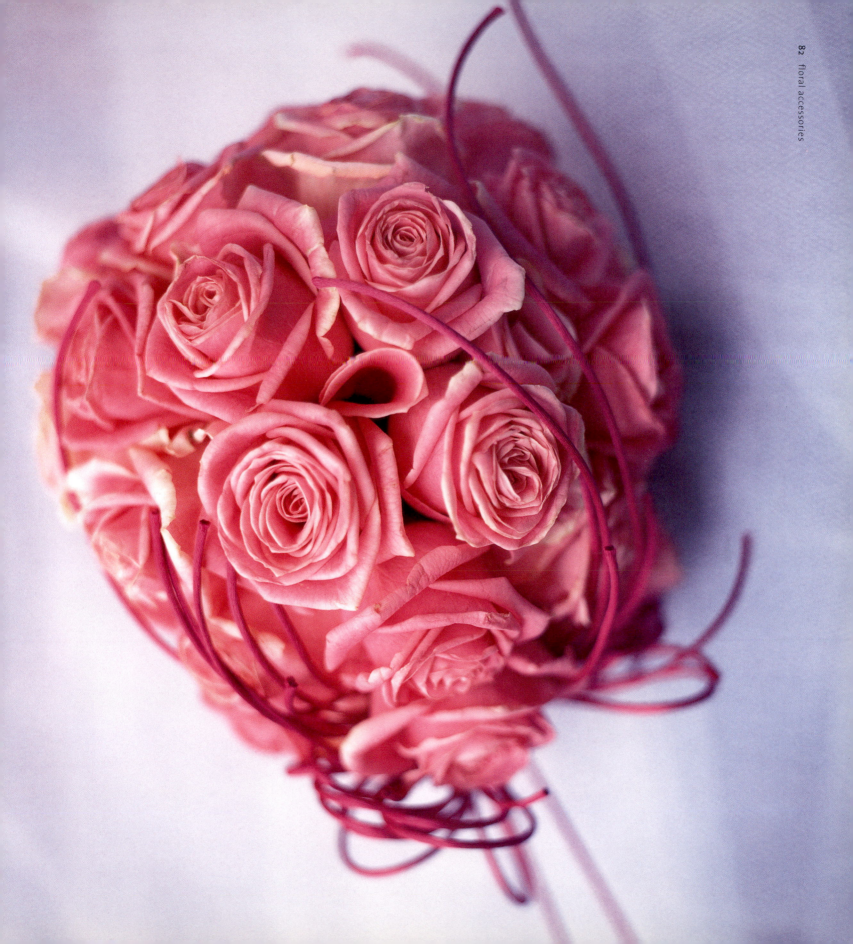

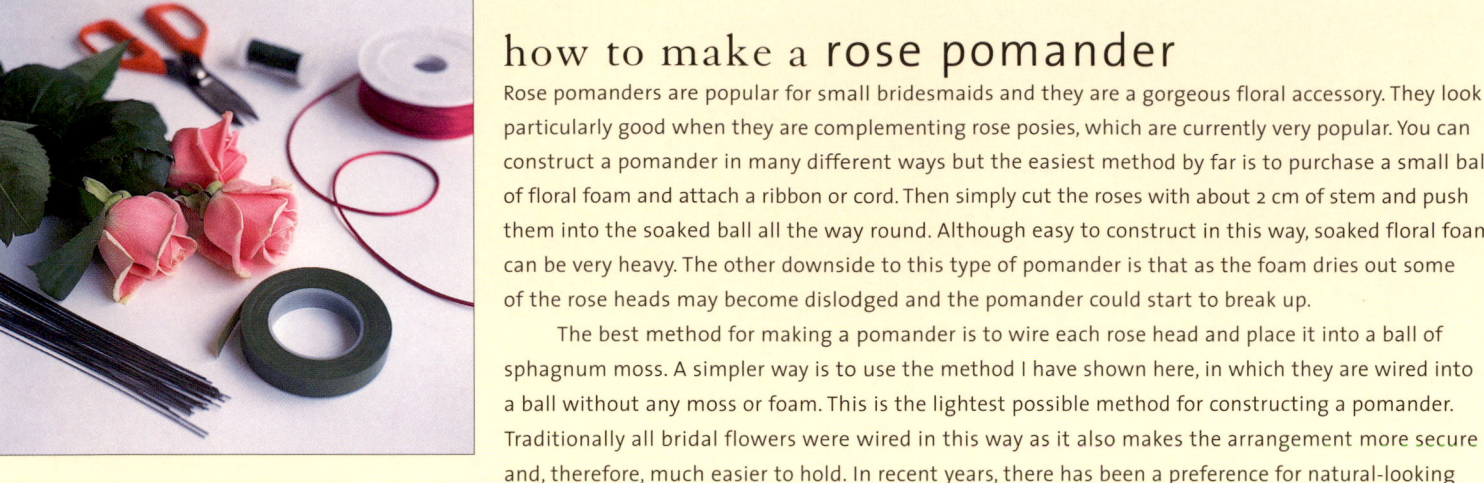

how to make a rose pomander

Rose pomanders are popular for small bridesmaids and they are a gorgeous floral accessory. They look particularly good when they are complementing rose posies, which are currently very popular. You can construct a pomander in many different ways but the easiest method by far is to purchase a small ball of floral foam and attach a ribbon or cord. Then simply cut the roses with about 2 cm of stem and push them into the soaked ball all the way round. Although easy to construct in this way, soaked floral foam can be very heavy. The other downside to this type of pomander is that as the foam dries out some of the rose heads may become dislodged and the pomander could start to break up.

The best method for making a pomander is to wire each rose head and place it into a ball of sphagnum moss. A simpler way is to use the method I have shown here, in which they are wired into a ball without any moss or foam. This is the lightest possible method for constructing a pomander. Traditionally all bridal flowers were wired in this way as it also makes the arrangement more secure and, therefore, much easier to hold. In recent years, there has been a preference for natural-looking flower decorations and the more widespread use of floral foam has changed the way florists construct floral accessories. Wiring flowers in this way takes practice and I do not recommend attempting to make a rose pomander for your own wedding without practising several times first!

MATERIALS

40 roses (such as 'Vendela Rosita')
50 x 0.71/22 guage stub wires
50 x 28 silver wire
Gutta-percha tape
0.32 (30 guage) binding wire
Ribbon
Scissors
Nimble hands and lots of patience!

STEP BY STEP

1 Cut off each rose head. Support each rose by placing a stub wire up the middle of the stem and a silver wire through the calyx to prevent it from twisting round on the stub wire. After you have wired and wire each flower head tape with gutta-percha tape.

2 Attach binding wire to the first rose and start placing rose heads together binding around the wires as you go.

3 Build up the pomander by bending each rose to its position and binding as you go. Work round the pomander building up layers and then working in towards the base.

4 When you have completed the pomander and just before the last rose is in position, cut off any long wires and tape over the exposed ends. Wire in the ribbon at this end and then finish off by adding the last rose, taping it to the other stems with gutta-percha into the middle of the pomander. Reposition all the heads to make the top perfectly round and mist with a sprayer to refresh the blooms and make them last longer.

how to make a dog collar

Many couples want to include their pets in their special day and, now that a huge variety of ceremony venues is available, it is becoming far more common to include a dog – or even a horse – in the wedding celebrations. We have made several floral dog collars for our canine friends as well as floral decorations for horse halters.

The easiest way to make a dog collar is to take a fabric collar and bind your flowers around this. If you can't find professional floral wires you can create a very basic version by tying a few robust flower heads to some ivy vines and attaching these to the collar. For a more sophisticated version you will need a variety of heavy wires and some gutta-percha tape as well as some sturdy flowers. I prefer roses, hydrangeas, orchids, gerberas, amaranthus, berries and mixed foliage, but I have made them with delicate flower heads such as gloriosa and ranunculus. (Here I have used 'Grand Prix' roses as they are lovely, chunky and strong.) The most important thing to do is to make sure that the floral collar is comfortable for your dog. The first thing he will do if he feels irritated is roll and that will certainly crush the flowers. This is why I think the safest and best way to create an arrangement like this is to wire it onto to a collar that your dog is familiar with and that fits well. Once fitted, gently spruce up the flowers. Tell your dog how handsome/pretty he/she looks and instruct not to roll!

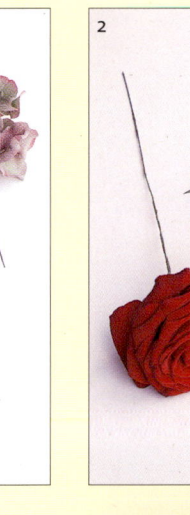

MATERIALS

12 roses (such as 'Grand Prix')
12 branches of skimmia foliage
3 large hydrangea heads.
Stub wires (0.90mm/20 guage and 0.71mm/22 guage) and silver wires (0.32mm/30 guage)
Gutta-percha tape
Scissors
A fabric dog collar

STEP BY STEP

1 Cut off each flower head and add a supporting wire. Wire each rose internally by inserting a 22-guage wire through the stem and into the calyx (the very base of the flower head). Add a silver wire through the calyx and secure it onto the main stem wire. Single-leg mount the skimmia with a 22-guage wire and the hydrangeas with a 30-guage silver wire. (Place one wire along the stem and wind the other leg over it three times.)

2 Tape with gutta-percha from the top of the wire to the bottom. This helps to protect the flower, keeping in moisture.

3 Measure one 20-guage wire around the dog's neck, to tape the flowers onto. Cover the wire with gutta-percha tape first to hide any joins.

4 Add the flowers and foliage, piece by piece, alternately using gutta-percha to secure; start at one end making a hook first. Cut off any unnecessary wires as you tape along. Finish the collar with another hook to act as a clasp and secure it in place. Wire onto the outside of the collar, adjust the fit and talk sweetly to your dog!

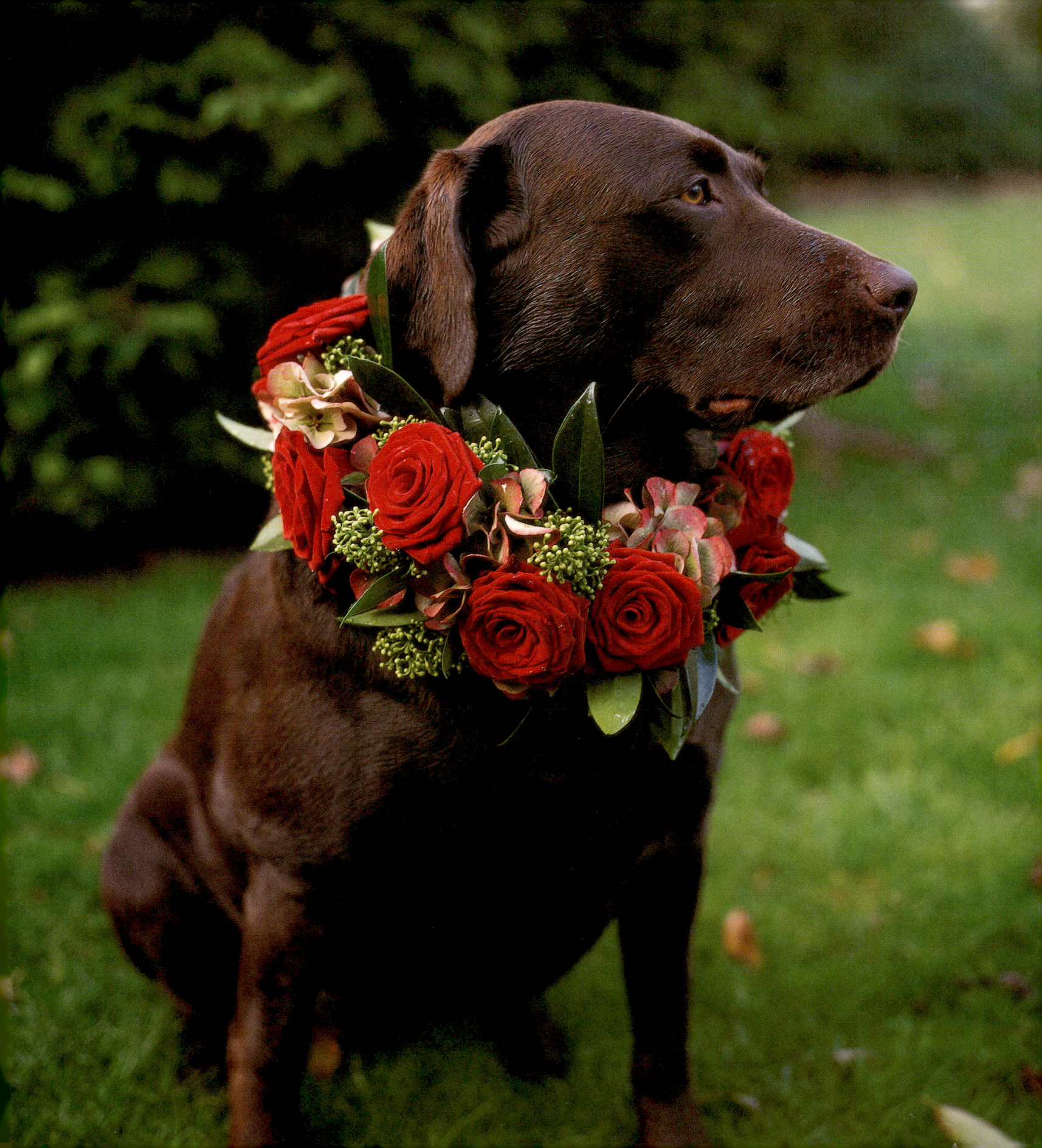

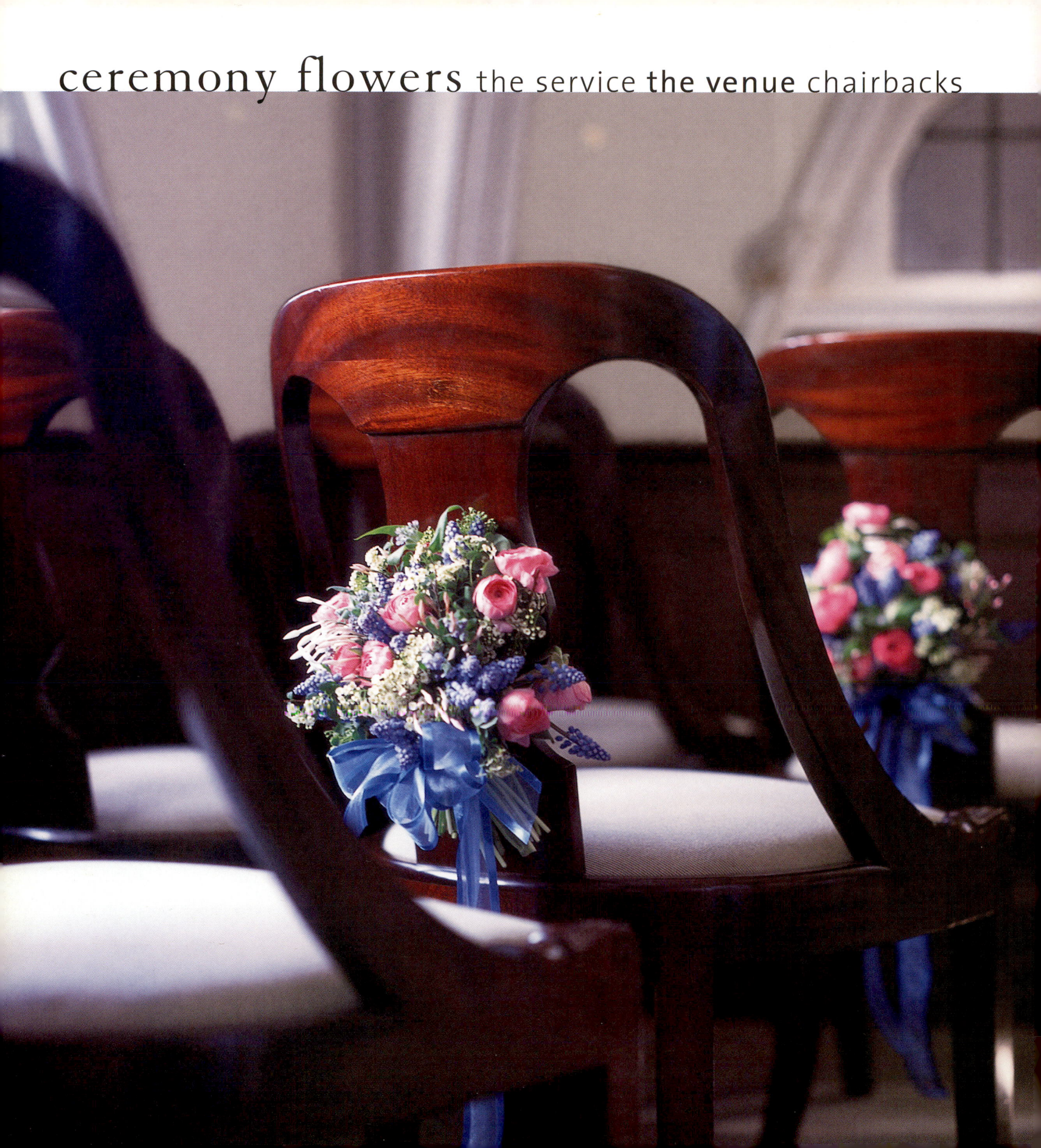

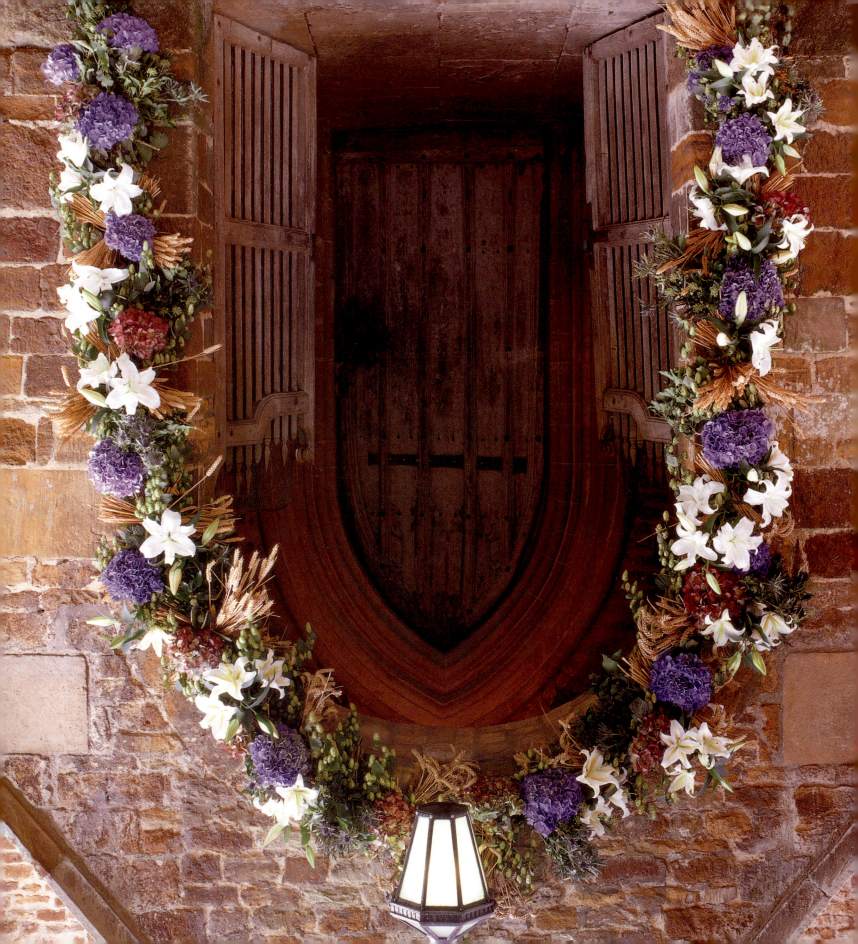

the style of service

There is a well-known Chinese proverb that says that a journey of 10,000 miles begins with a single step and as you start to plan your wedding, you may be able to identify well with this. Making the initial and crucial decisions about the date, the venue and timing can seem very daunting and more difficult than you expect. Whatever the venue or timing, flowers are the perfect way of creating the right atmosphere and enhancing the ceremony, and with a little planning you'll find the perfect floral arrangement to suit your needs.

the venue
Having set your date the next thing to do is to decide on the location and time of your ceremony. Traditionally the wedding is held close to bride's home, but if the bride and groom are arranging the wedding themselves they may choose a place that is special or local to them, especially if the bride has been living away from home for many years.

The ceremony is the soul of the wedding, where you and your fiancé pledge your love for and loyalty to one another. Wherever you choose to hold your ceremony there will, at some stage, be an exchange of vows and this is the spiritual part of the day. The specifics of the ceremony will depend on your beliefs and preferences and you may well have the opportunity to make this unique to you. Due to the immense range and style of wedding ceremonies the choice of decoration also varies enormously. It may be that you have for a backdrop the hillside beside an English castle, a Venetian Palace and the Grand Canal, a chapel in Las Vegas or a ruined church on a clifftop. Flowers will enhance any venue. Whatever your religious preference and budget there are certain ways that you can make a service more spiritual. The use of candles outside the venue in storm

lanterns or inside on stands adds ambience. Even if you do not have a traditional place of worship you may wish to simulate an aisle or have your guests in a circle with you and your groom in the centre.

Couples watching their costs may decide to forego the expense of ceremony flowers and spend their resources on flowers for the reception, which will of course be enjoyed over a longer period. Alternatively, they may choose arrangements that they can take on to the reception and get the benefit of them for longer. There are limitations to this as large flower arrangements do not travel well and you may require your florist to move them for you – this will incur added transport and labour costs on the day. For one outdoor wedding picnic we arranged huge high-handled flower baskets containing scented stocks so that the guests could literally carry the decorations and the fragrance with them.

marrying outdoors

When planning an outdoor wedding it helps to think like an architect or a theatre designer. Make sure that everyone can see and that there is adequate seating and protection from the elements. If you are on a limited budget then have one large arrangement on your altar or by the celebrants' table or just decorate the top outside edges of the chuppah.

One of the most effective outdoor wedding ceremonies I have seen had just one huge urn of pale pink hydrangeas and an aisle scattered with pale pink rose petals. The aisle was closed off with ribbon until the bride and her father arrived so that the guests entered via the outer ends of the rows of chairs, making the rose-petalled path sacred to the bridal party. In civil ceremonies, flowers can be an important part of the proceedings, for example being offered to your new family. Sometimes single roses are given to each of the new parents, uniting the family in joyous celebration. This custom has its origins in Asia, where leis are often offered as a symbol of unity.

choosing your flowers

The colour of your ceremony flowers may be determined by a number of influences. It may be the location you choose – if your ceremony is outdoors in the full summer sun then you may opt for brightly coloured flowers or rich colours that will stand up to the bleaching effect of bright sunlight. In the temperate climate of Britain the popularity of the all-white garden is reflected in the frequent choice of white-and-green colour schemes for wedding flowers; both trends are influenced by a need to work with lower light levels. White and lime green are quite luminous together and work well in dark churches.

Apart from the light and the weather conditions, traditional or cultural beliefs may inspire your wedding colour choice. In China, red and fuchsia are considered lucky and the colours of marriage and good fortune. The luck associated with the humble shamrock in Ireland makes green the colour of good luck and fertility. In India, where colour plays an essential past in the Hindu religion, brides are sprinkled with yellow turmeric, yellow and gold clothes are worn and even yellow food is consumed to bring good fortune and health to the bride and groom. Or the colour you choose may be distinctly personal – you may think of red as the colour of love – or you may just select your favourite colour to make you day special.

OPPOSITE Formal photography has been less popular recently as more couples have chosen to have reportage style photographs. Although this large group, photographed outside St Paul's Cathedral, will have taken some time to organize, it's a good way of making sure that you've got a picture of everyone who came to the wedding.
RIGHT Ask your photographer to take some pictures of the ceremony room before the guests arrive so that you've got a good record of how your flowers looked on the day – you will undoubtedly be too busy to do this later.

flowers in a church

Many churches can be magnificent buildings in themselves and a few well-chosen flowers will increase the sense of occasion and pleasure. The flowers do not have to be costly or elaborate and a few jugs of scented blooms in a small country church can look charming. When planning the decoration for a medium-sized church with a limited budget it is better to have one or two major displays rather than lots of small arrangements dotted around the place which will tend to get lost in their surroundings.

The larger the church, the more important the scale of any flower arrangement you include is, so if you are planning to hold your nuptials

in a cathedral think grand! If you really want to go to town and have a very flowery ceremony then list all the places you would like flowers and see what fits the budget. It is especially welcoming to greet the guests with flowers at the entrance. Some churchyards have metal archways across gates where flowers can be attached, or swags can easily be attached to lychgates. The doorway to the church itself is a great place to construct an arch of flowers, which then becomes a fantastic frame for the photographs. But if the budget will not stretch that far, then place some small flower arrangements in the alcoves to welcome the guests inside or topiary trees on either side of the door.

BELOW In Jewish weddings the ceremony takes place under a special canopy known as a chuppah. Here a cream canopy has been decorated with four floral swags that have been tied to each of the posts. A chuppah is set up on the morning of the wedding and is not a fixture of a synagogue. This means your florist will have to arrange your flowers on the morning of the wedding, not before.

Once inside the church I think the focus for flowers should be the altar and depending on the size of the church it is good to have one or two large groupings of flowers here on tall pedestals. Remember that most of the service takes place between the pulpit and the lectern at the chancel rails. If the budget allows them, my next priority is for pew ends on every other pew if the furniture suits this and, if it does not, I like to add candle stands to frame the aisle. The aisle is the focus of attention for the processional when the bride arrives and the recessional when the newly married couple lead their guests from the church, and so is one of my favourite places to decorate. Of course there are masses of other possibilities such as flowers in the font and flower arrangements at the base of every window. The different architecture of individual churches will offer other ideas for decoration from screens within the church to collars around each pillar. It is always lovely to have some sort of floral decoration actually on the altar too as this is where the happy couple finish their prayers before the recessional.

Most churches have a few church flower arrangers and you will know from what you see during your banns what level of skill they have. Some churches have bands of very talented and enthusiastic flower arrangers who can do wonders with a few flowers and are often very generous, cutting additional plant material from their garden, but others are very amateur and

you may not wish to consider them for your decorations. For my own wedding I wanted to have flowers simply everywhere and so enlisted the support of the church flower arrangers as well as using professional florists for some of the key areas of the church. I was married when I was serving my apprenticeship as a florist before I had my own business and I have to say the church flower arrangers did a very beautiful job. I was lucky enough to marry my husband Peter in the same church where my parents were married and so it was lovely to work with local people we had all known for a long time. Whatever your situation, you will need to find out who is in charge of the flowers, as some churches do not allow outside florists and have a preferred team to work with.

It is also prudent and polite to check if there are any areas where you cannot have flowers as individual clerics have their own views. It is also a good idea to find out whether there is another wedding on your chosen day as this may mean that you can share the costs of the flowers. Do remember if you are planning a wedding during Lent your vicar may restrict you to just bringing in flowers for your ceremony as flowers are

not generally displayed in churches during this time. Remember too that in Advent the church may have a lot of its own decorations, including a nativity scene.

The Christian calender may influence the colour of flowers displayed in a church. For example, yellow and white flowers are traditionally arranged in Easter. The only other considerations to bear in mind are the altar cloth and any carpet, which may affect your choice of colour. It is customary to leave the wedding flowers for the enjoyment of the congregation for the Sunday service.

jewish ceremonies
Officiated by a rabbi, Jewish weddings can take place almost anywhere as long as they are beneath a chuppah. Some brides like to create their own chuppah from tulle or embroidered fabric. Others ask florists to create an arbour or floral canopy and these types can be especially effective for outdoor weddings. Over the years I have had the pleasure and honour of making many different styles of chuppah – from an iconic frame fashioned only from gardenias to a fantasy tulle chuppah with pink roses and a rustic birchwood frame for a country wedding.

As the canopy is not fixed and is only set up in a synagogue on the day of the wedding it is advisable to use a professional to decorate this. Normally floral decorations are hung at the top of the four poles. Sometimes the poles are garlanded and occasionally they can be totally covered with more elaborate decorations. If the budget allows, two larger arrangements may be placed at the arc of the synagogue and a trailing decoration included for the bima, where the register is signed.

flowers for civil ceremonies
A judge performs a civil ceremony and this can take place anywhere except a place of worship. In some countries (like Britain) the area or place has to be licensed to hold such an event but others (like the United States and Australia) are much more liberal about this and you can get married wherever you like. Civil ceremonies can be

ABOVE (CLOCKWISE FROM TOP LEFT) This traditional white-and-green arrangement in a formal verdigris urn is perfect for a simple church service; Garlands for columns are time-consuming to create and will require a site visit by your florist. This white-and-green garland with a Caribbean theme has been created by attaching floral foam cages to the top of the column and then arranging the flowers all around; Scattering petals to mark out the route for the bride is a fragrant and pretty way to start the ceremony.

just as spiritual and moving as religious ones, of course, and they can be more personal as in some cases you have the freedom to write your own vows rather than be restricted to a prescribed wording.

The higher the ceiling in the ceremony building the grander any flower arrangements need to be, especially in terms of their height, in order to make an impression. It is better to have one grand arrangement in a large space than ten small insignificant ones. It is always tempting to want an abundance of flowers all over the place but always consider how the room will look when filled with people. One single large arrangement that can be seen by everyone will say a lot more.

sculptural style

classic white flowers

classic white flowers were given a contemporary twist for Natalie and Dariush's early spring wedding. Natalie chose to marry at home and so a large marquée was constructed in the garden of her parents' home. A Persian ceremony at home was followed by a Catholic blessing in the family church, then champagne and canapés in the garden before the wedding breakfast in the marquee. To complement her Vera Wang dress Natalie chose a simple dome of roses that was edged with dark green aspidistra leaves.

The flowers for both the ceremony at home and the church were full of white spring blossoms including cherry blossom, spiraea and lilac massed with ranunculus, stocks, lilies and roses. Natalie's attendants carried a mixture of blooms to continue the theme. Her chief bridesmaid carried a posy of lily-of-the-valley and roses. (May is the best and least expensive time for lily-of-the-valley as it is in season.) Her younger bridesmaids carried white sweet peas edged with guelder rose and galax leaves. The delightful flower girl carried a small posy of lily-of-the-valley. All the bridesmaids wore individually wired hair adornments so that the hairdressers could pin them easily into their hair. The groomsmen wore rose buttonholes with a star-shaped head of Persian tuberose. A pale silver fabric was chosen for the tables in the marquee, creating a very cool, chic look. As Natalie had a large wedding (with over two hundred guests) she chose to have five

ABOVE Natalie and Dariush on the way to church following their Persian ceremony. Natalie chose white 'Akito' roses in a neat rose dome, edged with folded aspidistra leaves. Dariush's buttonhole is, of course, a single 'Akito' rose. **BELOW LEFT** Natalie and Dariush beneath the canopy at the Persian ceremony. The room is decorated with masses of Persian tuberose and jasmine, creating a wonderful sweet scent. Huge vases are filled with calla lilies, blossoms and guelder roses and edged with the arched spring greens of Solomon's seal. The white-and-green theme creates a coolly sophisticated look.

different table designs spread across the marquee, resulting in flowers at different heights spread out across the venue. She chose sophisticated flowers, including amaryllis, orchids and calla lilies, that were combined with roses to create a very sculptured and very contemporary look.

The horseshoe-shaped top table was raised on a platform and decorated with tall vases topped with phalaenopsis orchids and pots of lily-of-the-valley. The tallest table arrangements were phalaenopsis orchids and calla lilies. Amaryllis trees made medium-height displays and cubes filled with plaited flax leaves, roses and cymbidium orchids created a third, lower display. Finally glass dishes were filled with the green 'Midori' anthuriums, papyrus and calla lilies. The tables were all decorated with candles surrounded by snake grass and votives. Napkin ties of flax and orchids for some tables and stephanotis vines and pips for the others created a very lush table setting for each of the guests. After the wedding breakfast, the dancing began and all the candles and votives were lit. Many more candles and nightlights were placed on conservatory stands around the edge and the star cloth above the dance floor created the perfect ambience for dancing under the stars!

ABOVE For the marquee, Natalie chose a mixture of tall, medium and low arrangements, as well as using glass dishes filled with flowers, to break up the expanse of the large space. The combination of orchids and calla lilies brings a striking and contemporary look to the blank canvas of the marquee. RIGHT A four-tiered stand of champagne flutes topped with an elegant arrangement of flowers and foliage awaits the start of the festivities. BELOW LEFT The top table is a horseshoe shape and is raised on a platform so that all the guests can see the bride and groom. It is decorated with masses of stephanotis vines and tall glass vases topped with phalaenopsis orchids. Pots massed with lily-of-the-valley are dotted along the top table. BELOW RIGHT The three-tiered cake is decorated with sugar calla lilies and surrounded by snake grass tanks filled with rose domes. The table is edged with stephanotis vines.

decorating the venue

Although you are only in the ceremony for a very short time it is essentially the heart of the wedding and flowers will be the most significant way you can personalise the space and create an ambience. If you decide on a religious ceremony then you will have to check with the priest, rabbi or minister as to what decorations are allowed. If you choose to have a civil ceremony it is likely that you may need a slightly larger budget for your flowers as you will be creating your own special atmosphere. Many traditional religious venues are beautiful and highly decorative and therefore require less decoration.

LEFT It has become customary to adorn a chuppah by decorating the four poles. Here floral foam cages have been attached to the front and back of the pole so that flowers can be arranged on the inside and the outside of the canopy. Trails of jasmine have been added to trail the length of the pole and provide scent for the bridal party. **ABOVE** Ceremony flowers are best displayed on plinths that make the flowers easily visible. Here a glass urn of late summer flowers sits on a silver leaf pedestal. The choice of flowers for a large arrangement should be bold, big heads such as hydrangeas and chrysanthemums with spires of moluccella and delphinium and trails of lisianthus and amaranthus. **OPPOSITE** A loose arrangement of spring blossoms, early tree foliage such as sorbus and white delphiniums and lilies make a lovely scented vase to welcome your guests.

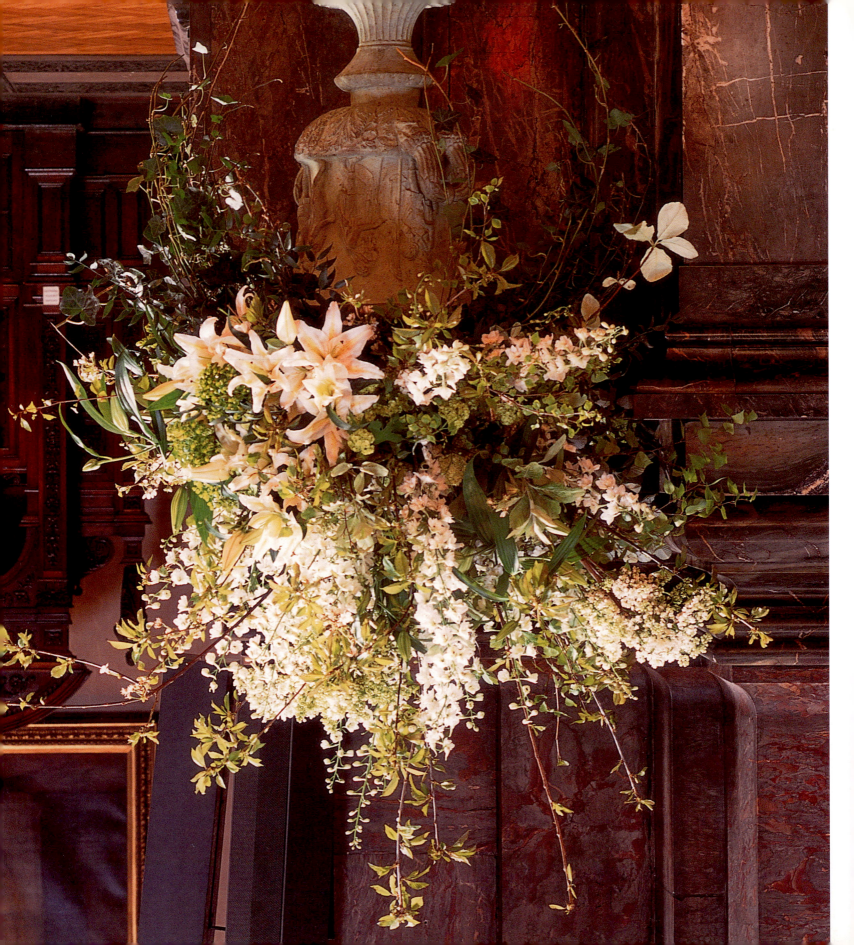

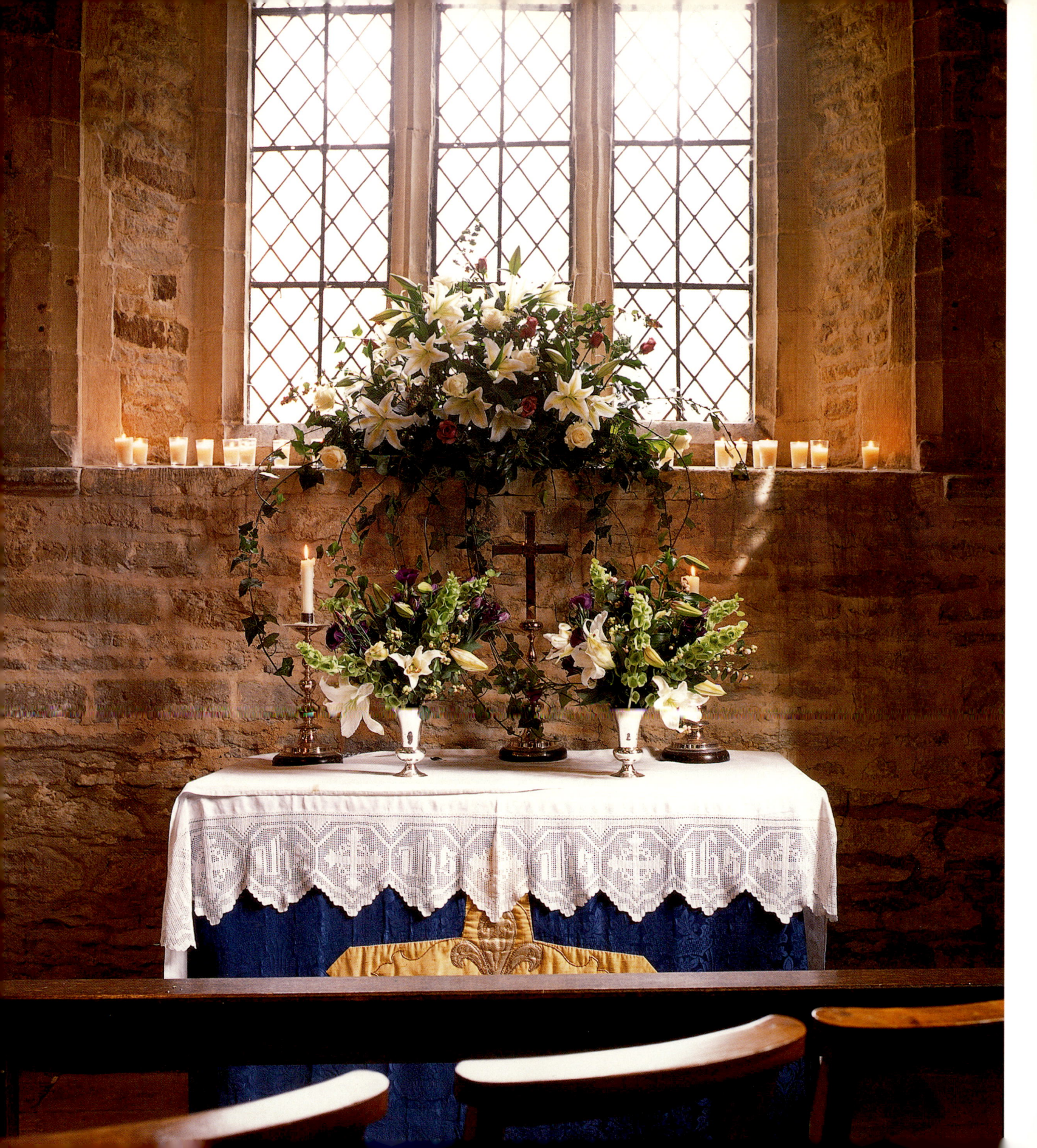

OPPOSITE With a small church, it is possible to decorate nearly all the windows and also the Lady Chapel. Here a trailing arrangement of lilies has been placed in the centre of the window with nightlights surrounding it. It is customary to use the appropriate vases that belong to the church for altar arrangements. **ABOVE LEFT** A trailing table arrangement of bright red gerberas, cymbidium orchids, alpinia gingers, moluccella and kentia palm leaves makes a perfect shaped display for the celebrants' table at a civil ceremony. Often this kind of trailing arrangement can then be moved onto the top table if you have a linear arrangement. **ABOVE RIGHT** A classic pedestal arranged for a wedding in Eltham Palace using vibrant red heliconias, alpinia gingers, 'Grand Prix' roses, moluccella, trailing amaranthus and lots of lush tropical foliage **RIGHT** Candlelight adds to the romance of any kind of ceremony. Decorations like these can always be moved on to the reception after the ceremony for maximum use.

chairbacks

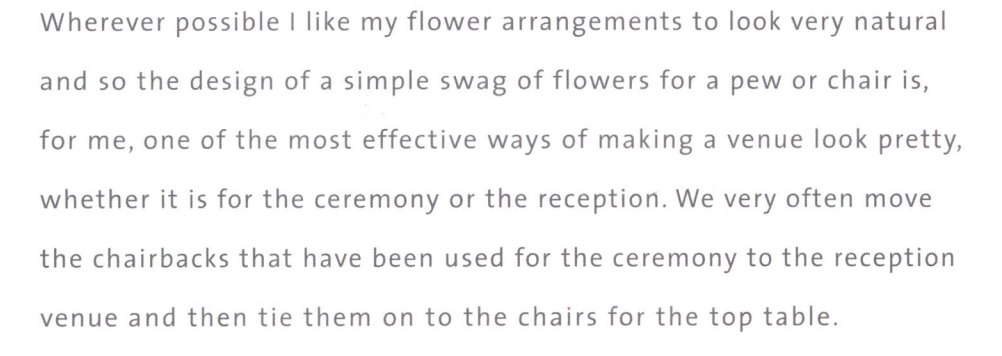

Wherever possible I like my flower arrangements to look very natural and so the design of a simple swag of flowers for a pew or chair is, for me, one of the most effective ways of making a venue look pretty, whether it is for the ceremony or the reception. We very often move the chairbacks that have been used for the ceremony to the reception venue and then tie them on to the chairs for the top table.

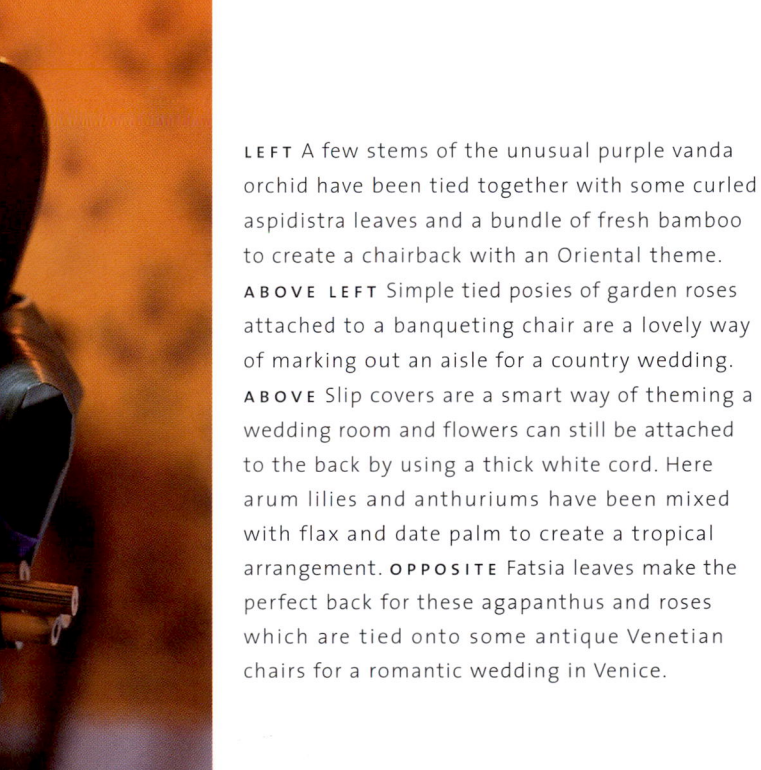

LEFT A few stems of the unusual purple vanda orchid have been tied together with some curled aspidistra leaves and a bundle of fresh bamboo to create a chairback with an Oriental theme. **ABOVE LEFT** Simple tied posies of garden roses attached to a banqueting chair are a lovely way of marking out an aisle for a country wedding. **ABOVE** Slip covers are a smart way of theming a wedding room and flowers can still be attached to the back by using a thick white cord. Here arum lilies and anthuriums have been mixed with flax and date palm to create a tropical arrangement. **OPPOSITE** Fatsia leaves make the perfect back for these agapanthus and roses which are tied onto some antique Venetian chairs for a romantic wedding in Venice.

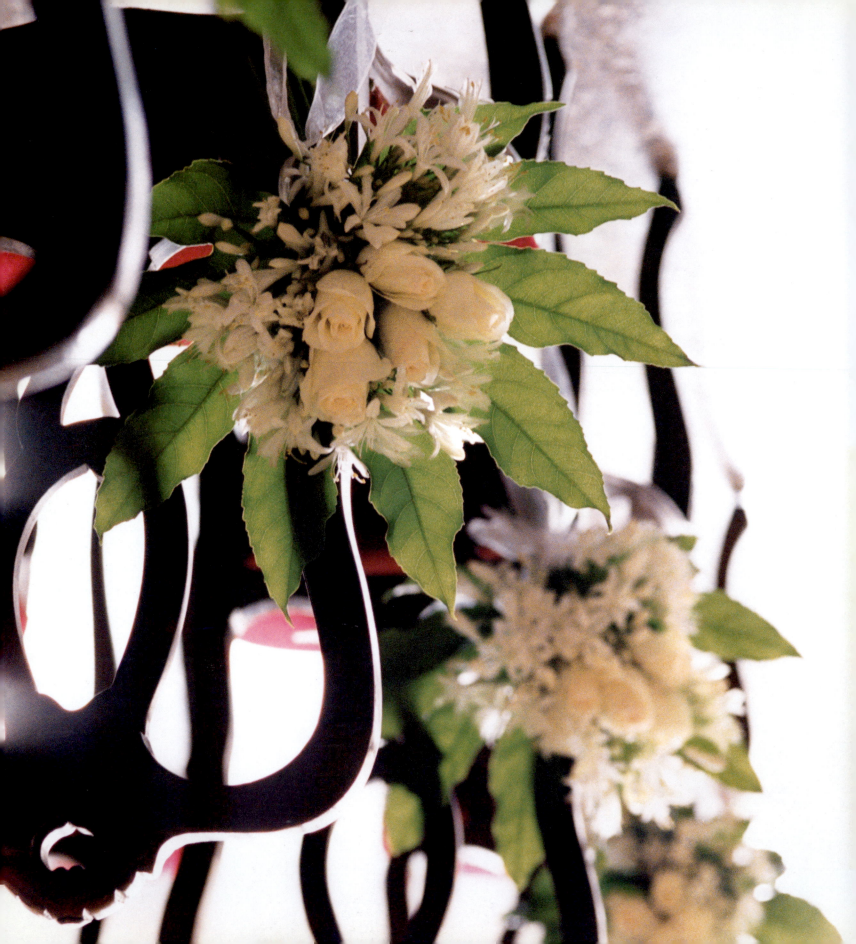

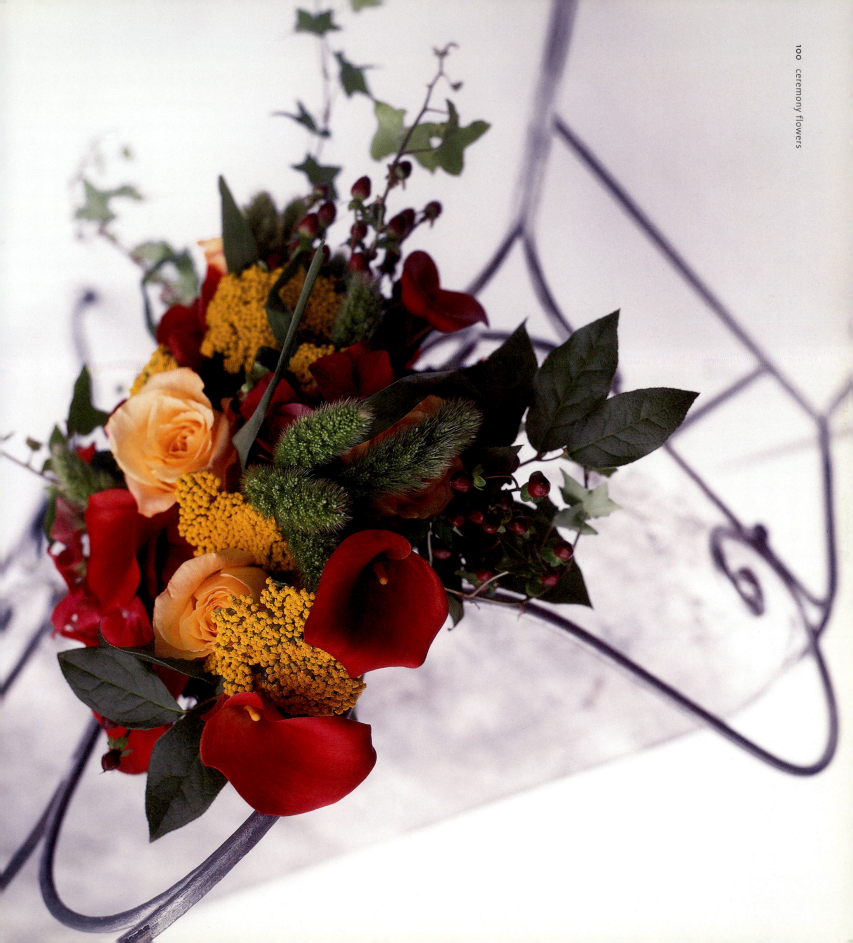

how to make a chairback

A chairback is essentially a tied swag of flowers that usually includes foliage. I love to incorporate these into my weddings as they are very pretty and add an informal touch to a ceremony. They are quite easy to make, especially if you use only one type of flower, such as gerbera, daisies or roses.

For a pew end or for a chairback for the centre of a chair you do need more skill to get a flat back to the display and a lovely elevated diamond shape for the flowers to look really good. The secret to success is choosing the right foliage and flowers. I normally use at least five types of foliage. You need something flat for the back like a branch of camellia, salal, beech, laurel or a large leaf like monstera. I like to add some textural foliage such as hypericum berries, poppy seed heads or hips and some fluffy foliage like *Alchemilla mollis*, grasses or branches of flower blossom in the spring time. Add a selection of pointed or long flowers such as calla lilies, roses, lysimachia and veronica and use round larger-headed flowers such as gerbera germini, open roses, dahlias, achillea as well as some trailing blooms, like lisianthus or amaranthus. Once you have made your decision on the choice of flowers it is essential to clear any excess foliage from below the binding point. (This is where you hold the hand tie whilst making it and it becomes the tie point when completed.) Once done, it may help you to lay the flowers out in their groups before you start, to make it easier to pick them up as you build the swag.

MATERIALS

Mango calla lilies

Millet grass

Achillea

Confetti roses

Salal

Hypericum

Ivy

Hydrangea

A length of tie and ribbon

Scissors

STEP BY STEP

1 First arrange your foliage, starting with the flat leaves at the back and adding more interesting textural foliage at the front to make a diamond shape. Feed some of the berries through to create some elevation to the swag.

2 Starting with the calla lilies place one towards the top of the hand tie to make the point of the swag. Feed in other flowers at different heights within the design, alternating from left to right.

3 Add the roses and achillea in the same way, pulling them down to graduate through the swag. Spiral the stems in the binding point will create a neat hand tie. The flowers will be shorter towards the binding point, but try to leave them long enough to stand proud and not appear squashed. The largest flowers should be the most noticeable and in the best position.

4 Attach the swag to the chair with a strong wire cord or binding wire and then make a three-looped bow to cover the binding point.

how to make a **heart wreath**

A simple heart wreath is a lovely way to accessorise a door or a gate for your wedding and because it is made using a wet floral foam frame it can be made a few days in advance of your special day. One of these would look great on a church door or gates, or at the entrance to your ceremony. Occasionally we create these for the bride's home to welcome her guests. Roses and orchids are excellent for this design because they last a long time and have regular shapes, but you could use hydrangeas for an autumn wedding, ranunculus for spring and sweet peas for the summer. When you are choosing the flowers and foliage for this wreath, look for colours that enhance each other. Here I chose the 'Black Baccara' roses because their colour co-ordinated so perfectly with the burgundy nose of the cymbidium orchid, and I chose skimmia foliage because it matches the rest of the scheme.

The ribbons from which the wreath is suspended are deliberately narrow so that they don't over-whelm the bouquet but you might choose to have a wider, more substantial ribbon or a selection of different coloured narrow ones to add something a little extra. Alternatively, if there is a strong and large enough hook on the place where you want to hang the finished wreath, you needn't worry about the ribbon at all. It is always worth considering how you are going to hang your wreath before you start decorating it because the position of the hook might affect how much ribbon you need.

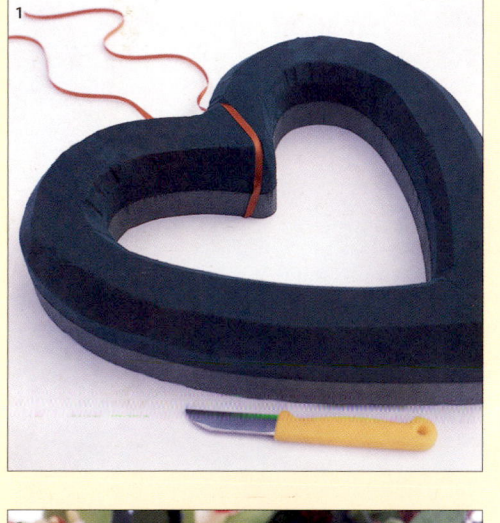

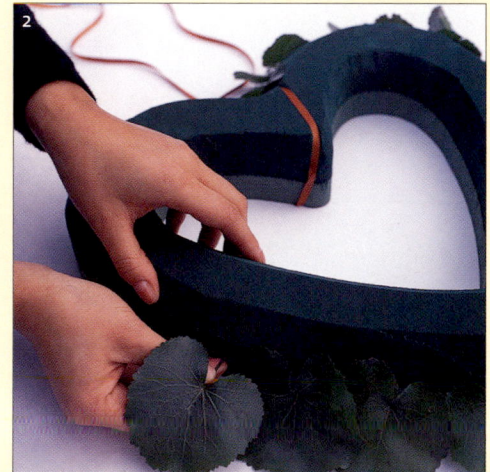

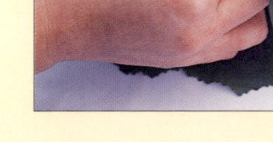

MATERIALS

1 x 45-cm-wide floral foam heart

1 knife

90 cm of 12-mm-wide red ribbon

Galax leaves

25 stems of red skimmia foliage

25 stems of large headed cymbidium orchids

60 'Black Baccara' roses

Floristry scissors or secateurs

STEP BY STEP

1 Soak the floral foam heart in a large basin for a few minutes until the bubbles cease to rise. Use the knife to trim the edge of the foam so that you can place the flower heads more easily to achieve a rounded shape. Fold the ribbon in half and tie the loose ends securely around the top of the heart.

2 Push the galax leaves into the foam around the outside edge and then across the front so that they are slightly overlapping each other.

3 Fill the front and sides of the heart wreath with the skimmia, which forms the base for the flowers. Cut each piece into lengths of 3–5 cm and then scatter evenly between the galax leaves. Position the orchids evenly around the wreath.

4 Finally carefully slot in the roses, filling the gaps between the cymbidium orchids and ensuring that you reflect the heart shape of the foam when positioning each one. When finished, mist the wreath and keep it in a cool place until you are ready to hang it.

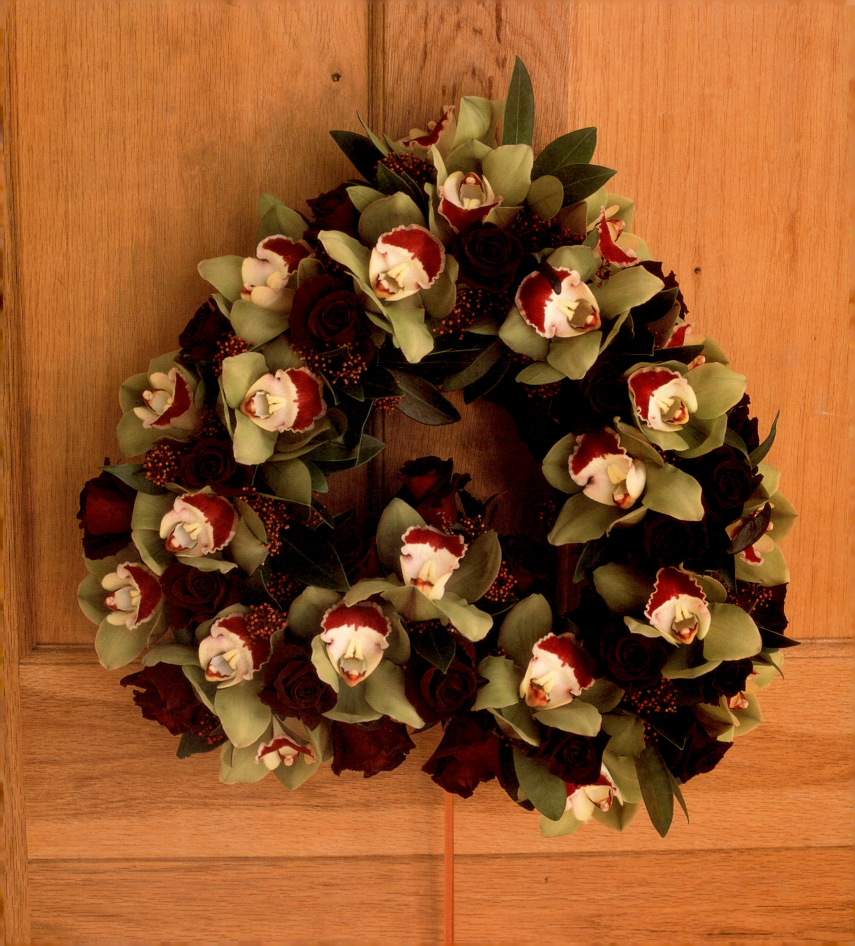

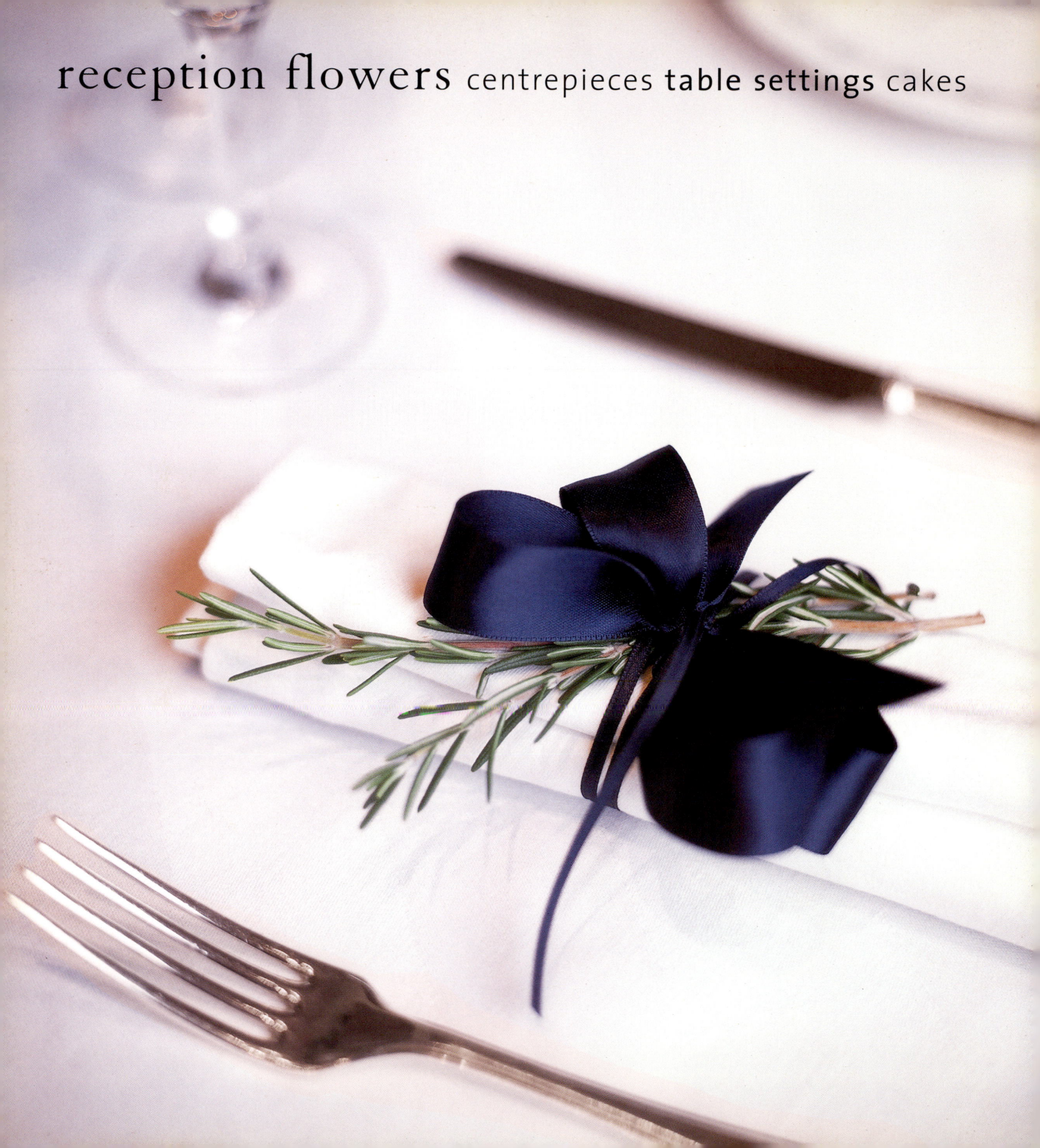

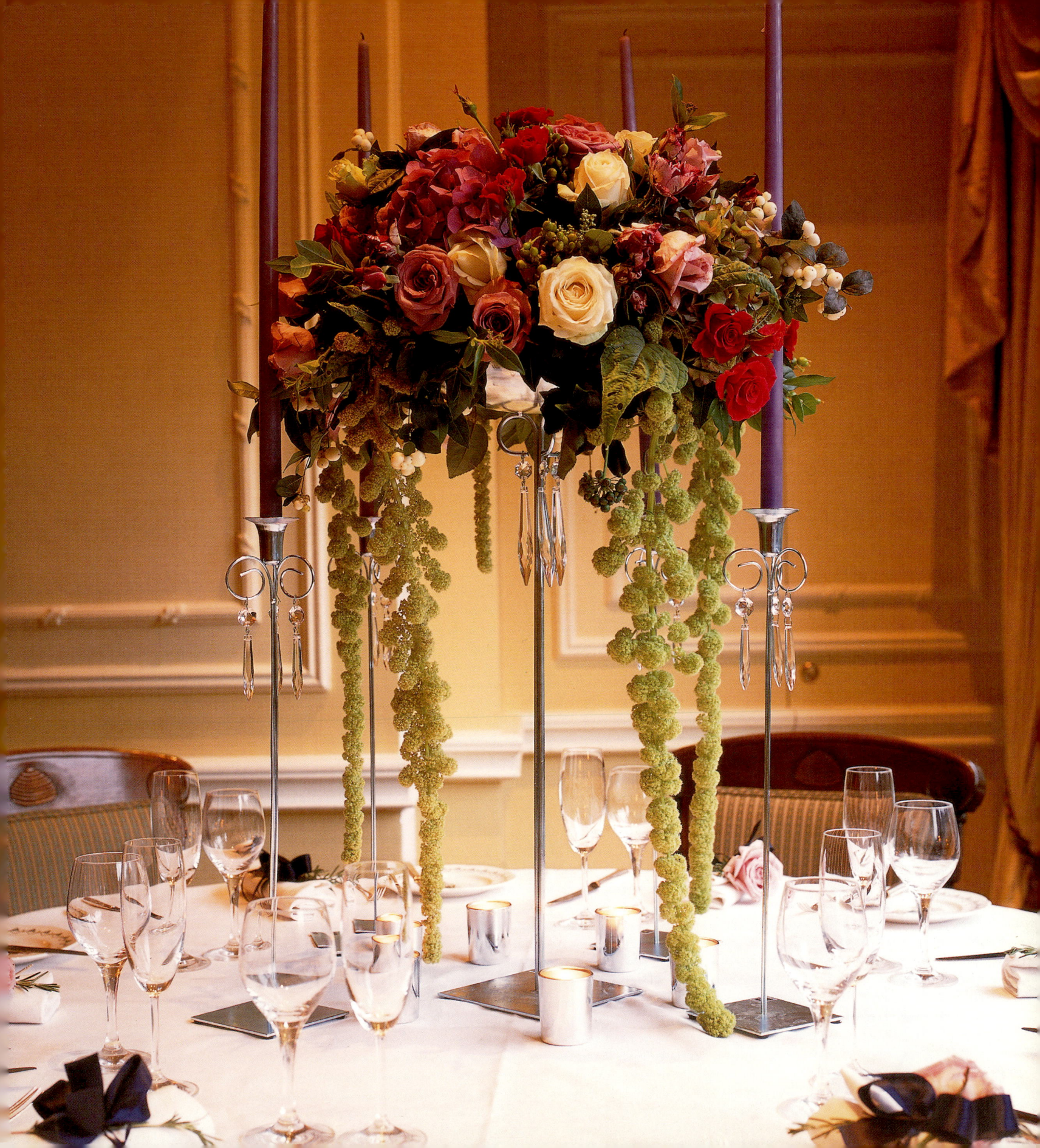

the **main** event

For most couples the reception is the party of a lifetime – it celebrates their marriage and marks the culmination of many months of planning. They want the reception to be unforgettable, to bring them together with their loved ones and to unite two sets of friends. When it comes to the floral decoration, the possibilities are endless, and, whatever the budget you are working to, it's possible to create a memorable and imaginative reception.

planning your reception

Your reception can be as unique as you want to make it – from an early wedding and a superb simple brunch to a late afternoon wedding or a lavish and elegant dinner dance. Most people go for the middle of the day and have an afternoon reception. Certainly limiting the length of your reception will help to curtail the expense. One option is to have an afternoon tea reception. Instead of large round tables you can hire smaller ones and use fewer table decorations and simple flowers for the table or even choose one striking plant such as an exotic orchid.

Traditionally the wedding reception was held in the bride's home or settlement. Over time this tradition has prevailed and it is still lovely to have a home wedding if practical. You do need to have adequate space and a home reception is a lot more effort and work for all members of the family. Providing services such as toilets and parking can become a logistical nightmare and cause tempers to be frayed. Over the years it became more common to hold the reception in a local hotel or hall but more recently there has been a trend away from

ABOVE Long narrow tables need linear style arrangements. This summer arrangement was created using a flat tray, floral foam and a mixture of pale pink peonies, purple sweet peas, sky-blue delphiniums, bright pink ranunculus, white mock orange (*Philadelphus*) and sprays of lime-green *Viburnum opulus*.

traditional sites towards informal and varied locations – museums, mansions or even zoos! But whatever your choice of site the three basic elements that contribute towards a successful and enjoyable reception are the decorations, catering and the entertainment.

the florist's role
For the decorations most florists today offer more than just flowers. Many can also advise you on the look of the tables including details such as hiring tablecloths, chairs and seat covers to help you to create the ambience you have in mind. Florists work so frequently with caterers and other related industries that they can often be a great source of recommendation as to who to call for a quote and who they enjoy working with. Florists will often work closely with the caterers in particular to confer on the canapé decorations, and to design the floral decorations for the food buffets. Often they will meet with you at your tasting to discuss the food and table decorations in more detail. They also liaise with cake decorators to ensure that the cake table perfectly complements the room.

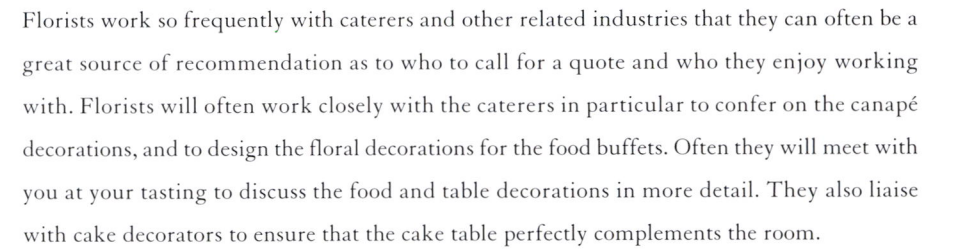

A creative florist will meet you at your chosen venue and will give you the best advice on where to place flowers and how many you should ideally have. Most often florists advise their clients to have fewer, rather than more, flowers but to go for grander displays which will be more striking when the party begins and the room begins to fill with guests. You also need to consider the installation and setting up of the room and the timings for this. Hotels may have more than one reception in a day, so you will be allocated a particular time slot that must be rigidly adhered to, or rented spaces may limit access times for your deliveries and services.

A florist's mission is to take your chosen wedding venue and change it into a room that is special and has the correct ambience for your wedding day. The blander the room the more you will need to spend on the decorations so think seriously about this when looking at your budget. Often a more expensive venue needs a lot less decoration and this can, in the long run, work out cheaper. Really formal venues do, however, necessitate huge and costly arrangements. Unusual venues may be more complicated for your contractors to work in. Stately homes and museums often limit your hours of parking and may be open to the public for part of the day, making the lead time for your caterer and florist very limited! If this is the case, it may mean that your florist does not have much time for complicated on-site arrangements and everything may have to be completed off site and positioned quickly.

Fragrance is very important at the reception. I think that it is essential to have some scented flowers, incense or scented candles at the entrance for your greeting line or cocktail hour. This is so evocative and the scents will always remind you of your special day. Do not forget to

ABOVE (CLOCKWISE FROM TOP LEFT)
Herbs are lovely to include in your wedding reception for their scent. Here, rosemary has been attached to a glass tumbler using double-sided tape to make a pretty, scented candleholder; A floral wreath for your door or entrance is a dramatic way of welcoming your guests to the reception. This wreath has been created using hydrangeas and white garden roses on a foam ring. Keep wreaths such as this cool and mist with water until you are ready to put them in place; A glass cube vase of white Avalanche roses filled with limes and edged with ostrich feathers makes a striking contemporary arrangement.

check out the rest rooms and add some lovely touches such as flowers and scented votives to make your guests feel pampered.

creating your theme

My favourite venues to decorate are marquees or tented receptions because they offer the florist a blank canvas to work from, but any room can be transformed to fit any theme with a little imagination and a lot of money! For example, one hotel ballroom was transported into a Moroccan palace with a club feel using brightly coloured fabric, a tented roof and swags of pea lights. Scented incense and fragrant flowers helped to set the scene further. On another occasion, to create a gypsy theme pieces of mirror glass were sewn on tablecloths of intense colour. A roving gypsy-style musical group worked the room and the flowers were jewel coloured throughout.

If your room is very decorative to start with lavish floral decorations may compete too much. Often the best schemes are monochromatic colours of cream and white flowers. This may seem like the obvious route to take but it does work very well and that is a reason for its endurance as a theme. It is classic and very beautiful. It can be made to look striking and minimal or romantic and blowsy. Fruit can also make a monochromic display more striking and add interest.

lighting

Your florist will also advise you on lighting – whether it be the addition of candelabras or votives to the table or getting a quote for a party lighting expert to make the best of your decorations. I cannot emphasise how important this is – the whole ambience of the wedding is determined by how comfortable and attractive the lighting is. Most ballrooms or spaces of a similar size have lighting that can be dimmed and each centrepiece can be spotlit from the ceiling, which greatly enhances the floral arrangements. Candlelight is flattering and the right lighting level makes everyone feel more confident and relaxed. If you decide to appoint a lighting company there are no limits as to what can be achieved, from uplighting floral arrangements to huge flambeaux for the entrance and a dramatic firework display for the finale. You will have an engineer on site all night to highlight your special moments, such as the cutting of the cake and the first dance. You may even choose to project images of stars and moons or decide to change the colour of the room through the clever use of light gels. Often these companies can also organise amplification systems if you are planning an especially large event.

chairbacks

Chairs are an important consideration too because there are so many of them in the room and generally there are very few designs – rental chairs are the same all over the world! It is a good idea to personalise at least the top table using chairbacks, tiny garlands of flowers or even a simple bow.

centrepieces

The practice of adorning tables with flowers, herbs and petals dates as far back as ancient Greece and Rome and has endured to the present day. The newly weds' table whether it be formal or round should be different and more opulent in look to differentiate the bride and groom from their guests. If you are having a large wedding with over 200 guests you may consider having some tall table arrangements to make the most of your space. It is currently very popular

BELOW A favourite design for an autumnal wedding reception using waxy deep red apples wired into a basket around a plastic dish filled with foam and then topped with dahlias, 'Grand Prix' and 'Milva' roses, rosehips, berries, skimmia and crocosmia. Alternatively for a white-and-green theme you could use 'Granny Smith' apples or use oranges to bring a vibrant colour to the table.

to have a mixture of half the tables set with tall arrangements and the other half low ones. If you are planning 300 guests you may even have three heights of arrangements. Tall arrangements are usually candelabras, topiary trees or tall glass vases so that the flowers are raised above the table. Usually the florist tries to raise these above the heads of the diners and the thin stem of the candelabra, tree or vase allows guests to see each other across the table. It is very difficult to hold a conversation with guests sitting directly opposite you on a round table because they are normally 1.5 to 2 metres across

and the ambient noise precludes this activity, but it is always more comfortable to be able to at least see across the table so bear this in mind when discussing the table flowers with your florist.

decorating the table
Table linen is very important. Most hotels offer white as standard but all caterers can hire in linen of many colours and shades. Standard colours and sizes are less expensive than cloths that fall to the floor in deep or rich colours. Personally I prefer linen to reach the floor. Your florist can help you choose a colour that complements your flowers and may even hire the linen for you. Napkins are a similar consideration if your budget stretches this far. You can have them trimmed with taffeta ribbon, have a bed created for an orchid or even use a sprig of herbs to decorate them and scent your tables. Place cards are normally co-ordinated with the linen and flowers as are the menu cards. Your florist and caterer will be able to recommend a calligrapher to help with these if necessary.

ABOVE (CLOCKWISE FROM TOP LEFT)
Scattering rose petals onto the card table is a romantic idea; An autumnal bar arrangement using the tomato-fruited egg plant (*Solanum integrifolium*) with black berries and lime-green balls of *Aschlepias physocarpa* in strong bands is topped with six savoy cabbages filled with confetti roses; A simple stacked cake, baked by the bride herself, has been decorated with flower heads and a small arrangement of flowers created in the bottom part of a white polystyrene cup. The bridal bouquet of lily-of-the-valley, alchemilla and garden roses has sensibly been placed back into a vase during the reception.

the wedding cake
The cake is the centrepiece of the reception and another area where you can let your imagination run wild, commissioning almost any design. In America the tradition is to also have a groom's cake, usually chocolate, and I think this is a lovely way of including the bridegroom. Often the theme can be chosen by the groom and it is a clever way of offering two cake options – a traditional fruit cake and a chocolate or sponge cake. The cutting of the cake (or cakes!) normally happens towards the end of the reception and the bride takes the knife and the groom puts his hand on hers. Often a wish accompanies this gesture and then traditionally they feed one another!

sophisticated city chic

a spectacular ballroom was the setting for Annabel and Stephen's wedding reception, after a ceremony at the historic Bevis Marks Synagogue. They shared the floral decorations for the synagogue with another bride and groom who were marrying before them, so I did not have the pleasure of arranging the flowers for their ceremony. I did organise the flowers for the reception, however. Annabel and her family chose a lime green, bright pink and lilac theme for the wedding and so a very romantic collection of flowers was chosen for the table centres and large arrangements. Annabel wore a delicious gold gown and she wanted to hold a simple hand-tied shower of orchids. To accommodate her wish, we were able to order a rare orchid from our specialist orchid grower that complemented the colour of her gown perfectly.

As the ballroom is large it suits having flower arrangements at several heights, including some tall designs to fill the space. All the arrangements included candles and masses of lit votives on the tables. The tall arrangements were placed in simple zinc stands adorned with crystals to match the magnificent chandeliers. The single candlesticks also sported dropped crystals making the tall tables very sparkly. The tall arrangements were created by using roses and hydrangeas in pink, lilac and green. The long trailing green plant is amaranthus, which can create a lovely sumptuous effect in tall arrangements such as these. The stem of the stand is thin so that guests can still see across the table and enjoy each other's company although it is usually quite difficult to talk across a table of twelve in a large ballroom! The medium-height arrangements were full mounds of roses, hydrangeas and lisianthus in lilacs and lime greens with a shot of bright pink. The low arrangements were floral rings encircling large glass bowls filled with lilac floating candles. Lilac candles were used throughout the whole ballroom and each napkin was tied with a navy bow to match the cupels used at the wedding. The men's napkins were decorated with a sprig of rosemary while the ladies had a 'Blue Gene' rose as well as rosemary.

ABOVE The bride and groom share a moment on their own. Annabel's hand-tied shower bouquet features phalaenopsis orchids, chosen specifically to match her golden gown. **RIGHT** The three styles of arrangement in the magnificent ballroom at the hotel. Grand venues like this benefit from arrangements of varying heights to break up the space. Matching candles, linen and napkin decorations complete the look.

ABOVE LEFT A few splashes of rain did not dampen the spirits of the bride and groom as – just married – they leave the synagogue for their reception. ABOVE RIGHT The card table is flanked with white phalaenopsis orchids with Italian papyrus grass in a tall lily vase. RIGHT This huge pedestal was created using many late summer blooms in pink, lime greens and lilacs. Bright pink 'Milano' roses and 'Medusa' lilies look fabulous with the spiky standard lime green chrysanthemums and big lilac ornamental cabbages. The trailing red flower is amaranthus, mixed with the green variety and lots of trailing ivies. BELOW The ladies' napkins are trimmed with a rose and a sprig of rosemary and tied with a navy bow.

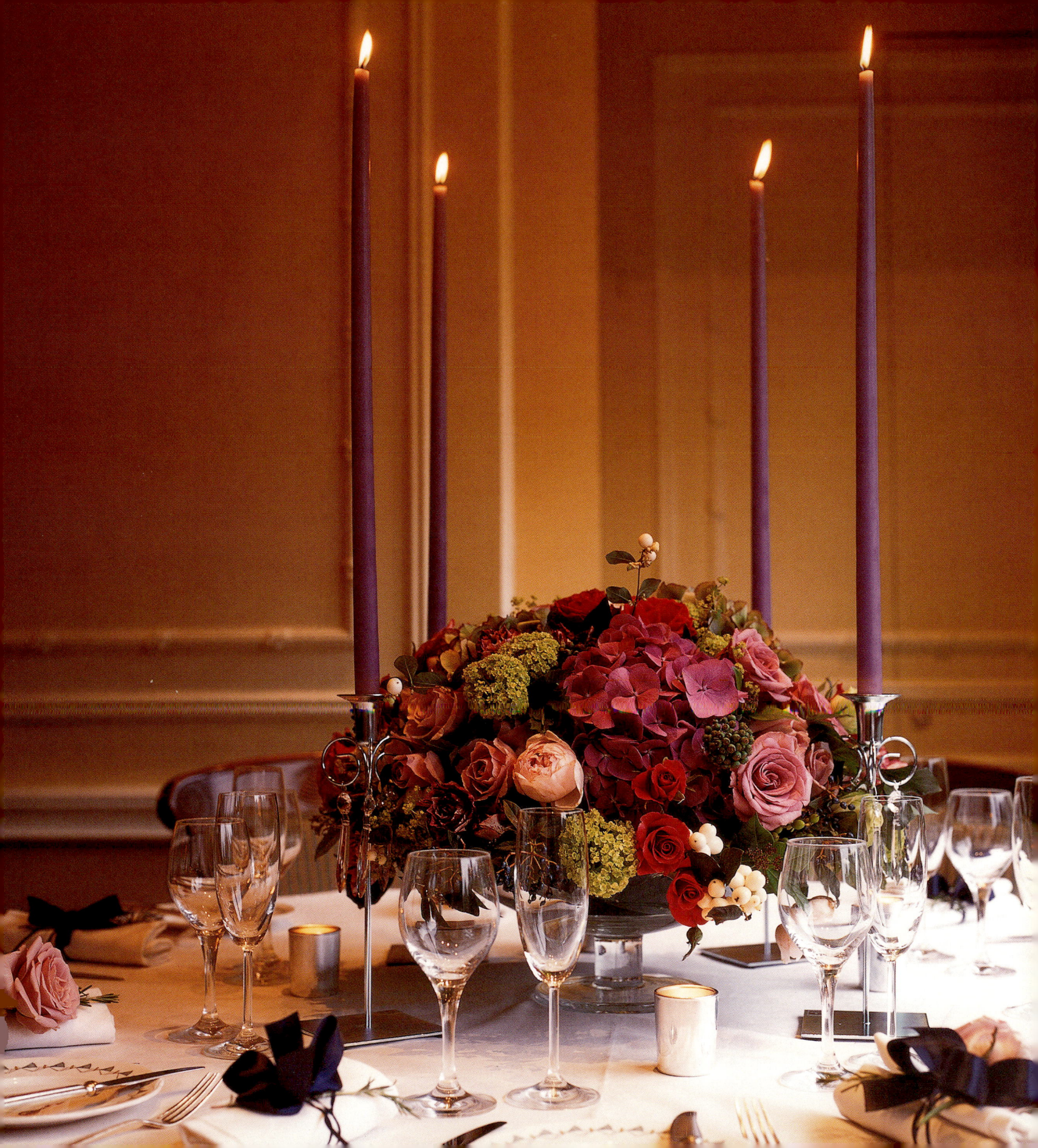

"Our day was simply perfect. Paula worked her magic and the venue looked spectacular."
ANNABEL

OPPOSITE Stemmed glass bowls have been lined with leaves and filled with flowers in the same pink, lilac and green theme. They are encircled by four tall lilac candles. TOP LEFT Individual cup cakes decorated with a lilac sugar rose were displayed on five tiers of glass and decorated with real lilac roses and rosemary. ABOVE, LEFT One of the tall arrangements – featuring roses and hydrangeas in pink, lilac and green. Trailing strands of amaranthus balance the height of the arrangement and the thin-stemmed stand doesn't obstruct the guests' view across the table. ABOVE, RIGHT The bride and groom stop for a photo in front of one of the large pedestal arrangements. LEFT Straight-sided glass bowls are edged with a floral foam ring and then filled with foliage and groups of roses and hydrangeas. Lilac candles float on the water to give a sparkly effect. BELOW The napkins for the male guests are trimmed with a sprig of rosemary and tied with a navy satin bow to match their cupels.

centrepieces

As food is the centre of any reception it is inevitable that your table will be the focus of the evening and your centre-pieces of paramount importance. Floral arrangements can be tall, low or differing heights depending on the size of your venue. You can use candelabras, topiary trees or vases and bowls, and votives and nightlights may be incorporated into your table-centre design. Flowers bring luxury, beauty and fragrance to the table.

OPPOSITE FAR LEFT A simple table centre to recreate at home uses a savoy cabbage as the base for arranging half a dozen 'Iceberg' roses. **OPPOSITE, TOP** A red square box and four tapered red candles are the basis for this contemporary arrangement which uses nuts and flowers in compact groups. **OPPOSITE, BOTTOM** This winter arrangement has been designed on a square ceramic dish and includes three frosted pale pink candles and six waxed and frosted pears. The delicate Easter lily has been mixed with tuberose and grey foliage (senecio) and a South African foliage called *Brunia albiflora*. **THIS PAGE** A vibrant lime-green and red theme was used throughout this autumnal wedding at Eltham Palace. This hand-tied bouquet is of ivy, red germini gerberas, 'Grand Prix' roses and cymbidiums.

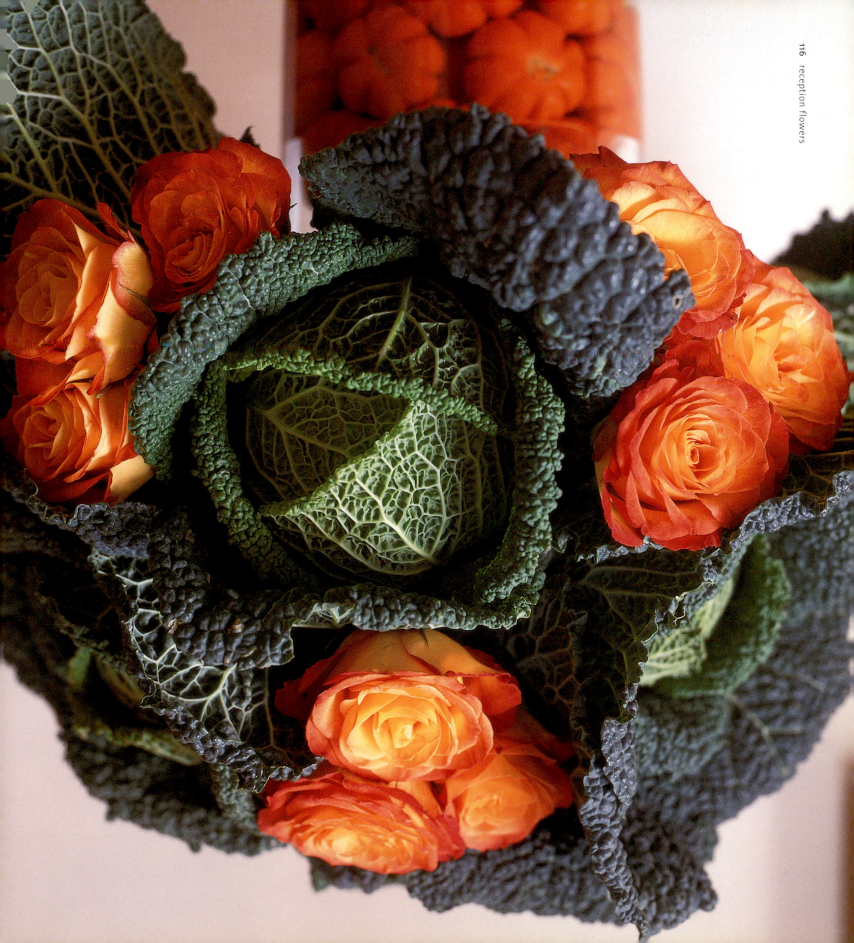

OPPOSITE I love savoy cabbages more as decoration than to eat because of their glaucous green colour which seems to complement any flower. They are also very textural and just by adding one or two roses you can make something that is quite simple look quite grand. **THIS PAGE** Another favourite tablecentre (which I use a lot in my own home because it is simple to create) features floating candles. Here three different height cylinders each contain one giant floating candle and are surrounded by a large floral foam wreath, filled with autumnal flowers, berries and apples, and encircled by votives.

THIS PAGE Flax (*Phormium*) leaves have been woven to create a basket-like effect inside a low glass cube vase. Arum lilies, cymbidium orchids, date palm and tropical leaves are arranged inside it for a table in a smart private dining room. The original inspiration for weaving leaves in this way came from a trip to Thailand. **OPPOSITE** Three giant fish-bowls have been filled with yellow calla lilies (*Zantedeschia* 'Florex Gold') with a tiny amount of water in each and then stacked on top of one another. This design works well with linear flowers such as tulips, phalaenopsis orchids and gloriosa.

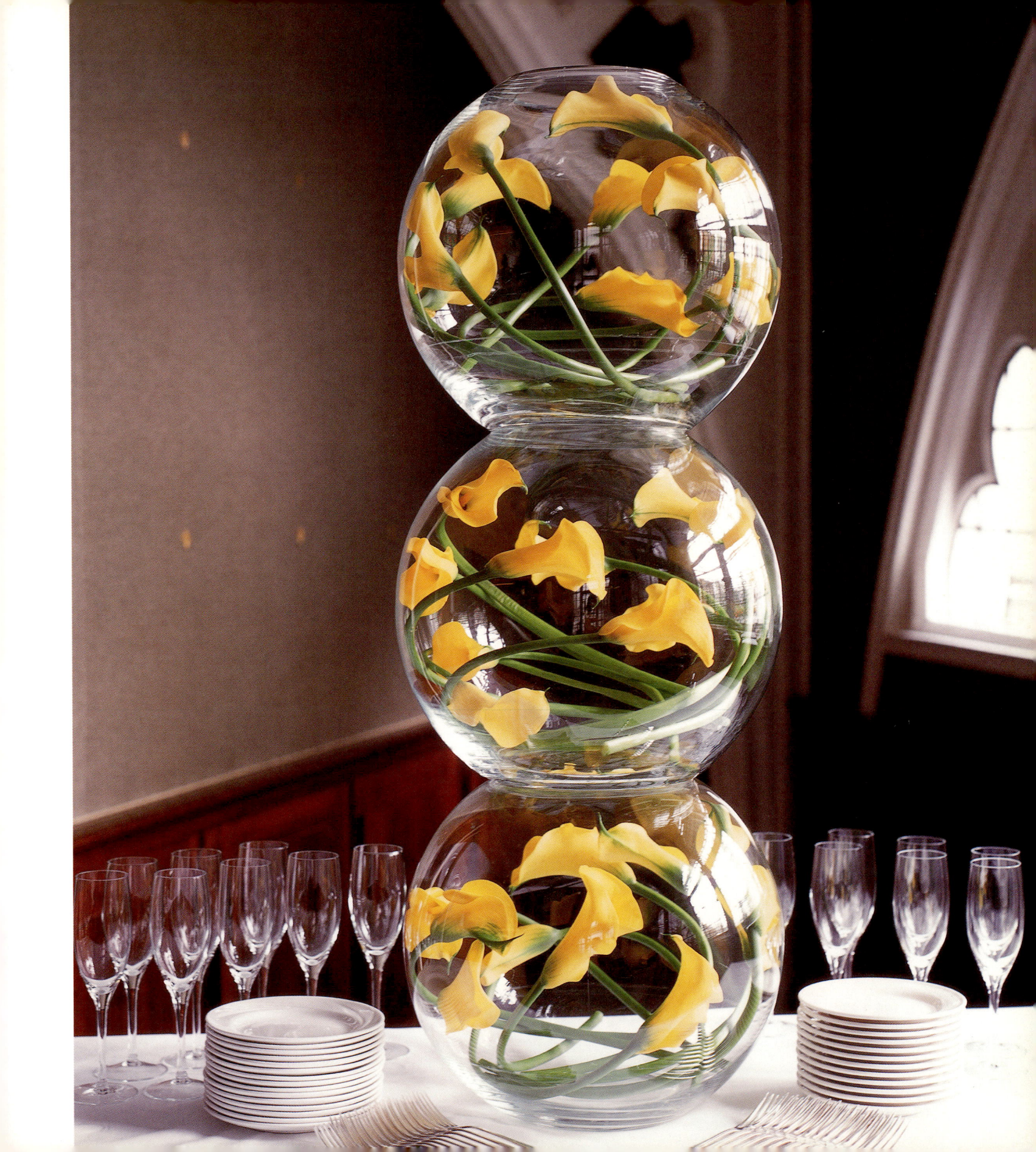

THIS PAGE, ABOVE AND LEFT The dark wood interior of the synagogue is enhanced with white and green spring blooms. The historic pews in the front rows are too delicate to sit on and so are decorated with garlands of ivy and groups of white 'Bianca' roses. Candlelight and traditional arrangements complemented the venue perfectly. **OPPOSITE, FAR RIGHT** Keren and Daniel preparing for their official photographs in a London garden square. Keren wore an elegant strapless dress with a small bolero for the ceremony because it is not considered appropriate to have bare arms in a synagogue. **OPPOSITE, TOP** Keren carried a round wired bouquet of stephanotis pips with some trails and edged with camellia leaves. **OPPOSITE, BOTTOM** Keren's beautiful dress was designed by London wedding gown designer, Ritva Westinius.

from traditional to modern

taking a different approach for the ceremony
and the reception made the early February wedding of Keren to Daniel an
extremely beautiful and elegant affair. The traditional decoration in the synagogue
contrasted with cool contemporary arrangements in a hotel, where the wedding
party feasted and danced the night away. Keren had a clear idea when we first met
that she wanted the flowers to be white and green, architectural, striking and modern for the reception, and softer and traditional for the ceremony. The synagogue is
a very beautiful candlelit venue and we filled it with early white and green spring
blossoms such as lilac, *Viburnum opulus*, prunus, *Euphorbia fulgens*, jasmine and
scented lilies. Jewish weddings are conducted under a canopy and it has become the
custom to decorate the four corners with hanging swags or garlands of flowers and
foliage. This is best done on site where you can position the floral foam and then
arrange the foliage and flowers around the pole. As the canopy is set up on the
morning of the wedding the flowers are very fresh. The white and green perfectly
complemented the simplicity of the building and were very fragrant. When the candles were lit, the ceremony looked truly magical.

For the reception Keren decided on 'living topiaries' of open white amaryllis
on huge glass dishes with large tropical leaves and textural seed heads for half of the
tables. For the others she chose very tall fluted vases filled to the ceiling with extra-
tall papyrus from Italy and sprays of white phalaenopsis orchids and 'Midori'
anthuriums. The use of two heights of table decorations for a ballroom gives height
to the room while allowing the guests to see across the table. Masses of frosted glass votives encircled the arrangements and each guest

was given a cymbidium orchid head, which was tucked into their napkin. The bride
and groom sat at a table for two with tables for their respective families on either side
and the table was decorated with a trailing arrangement of euphorbia and orchids.
Monstera leaves decorated the card table and a huge working fountain was placed in
the foyer and decorated with orchids to welcome the guests. The buffet tables were
decorated with glass vases filled with Brussels sprouts and savoy cabbages filled with
roses and orchids. The arrangements throughout the hotel were contemporary using
large glass vases and pedestals of perspex filled with pussy willow and blossom.

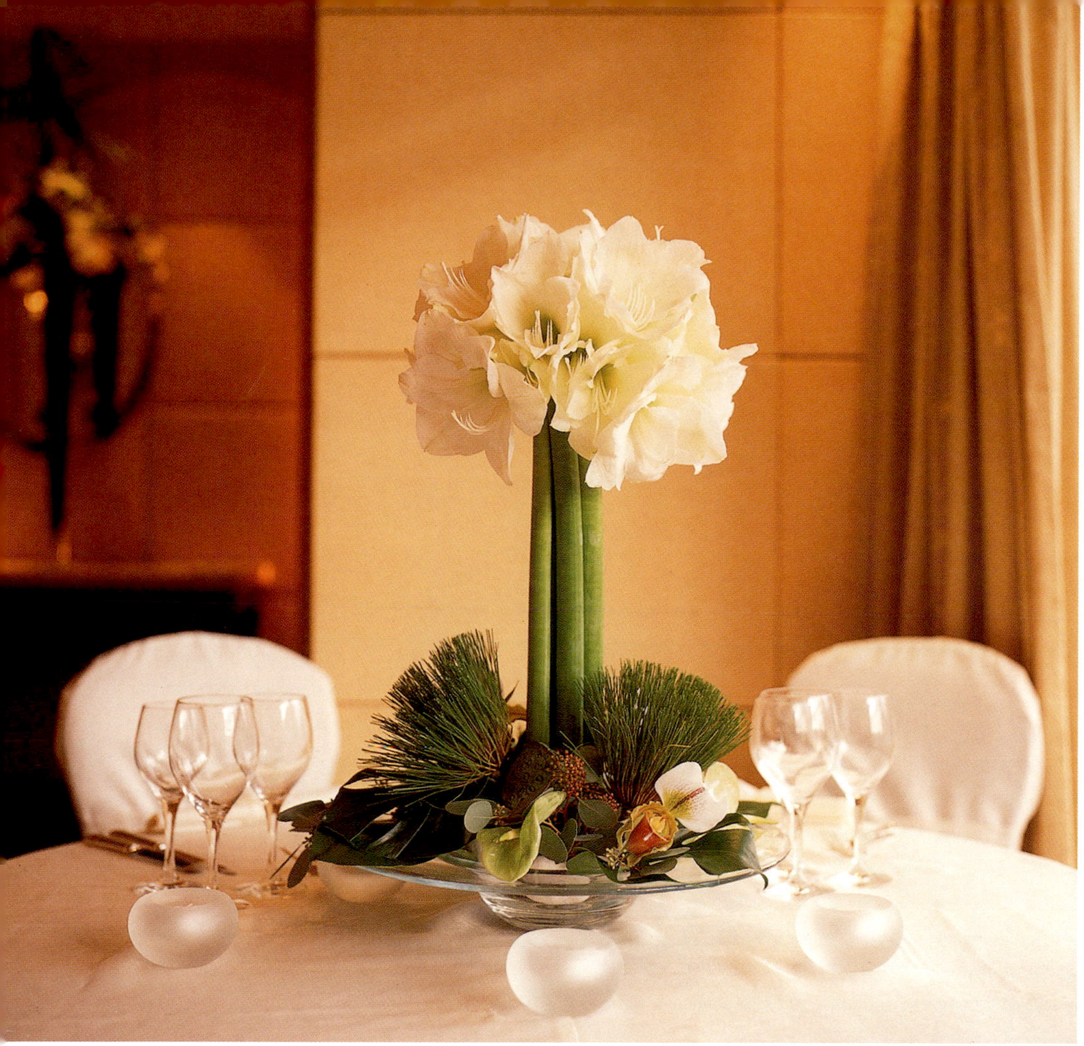

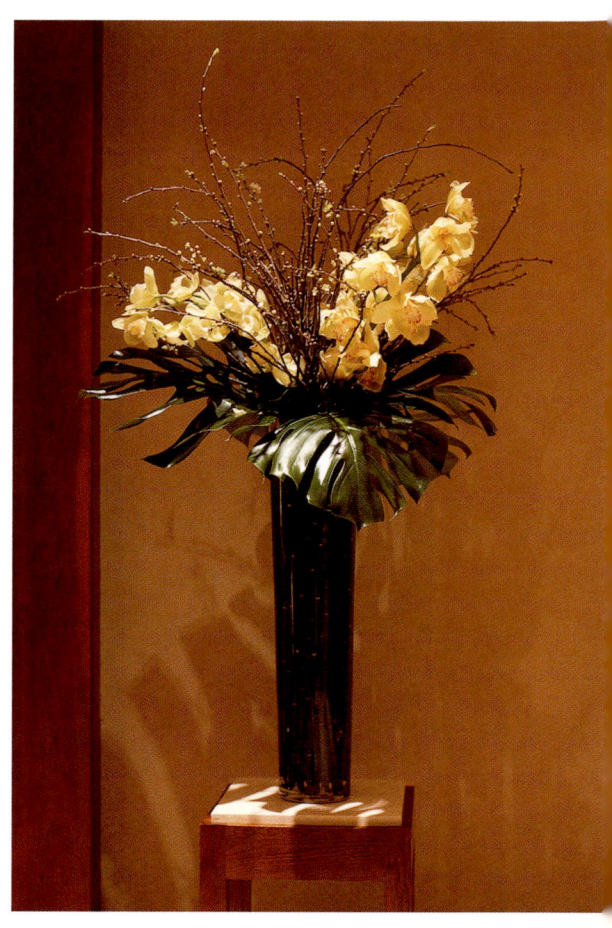

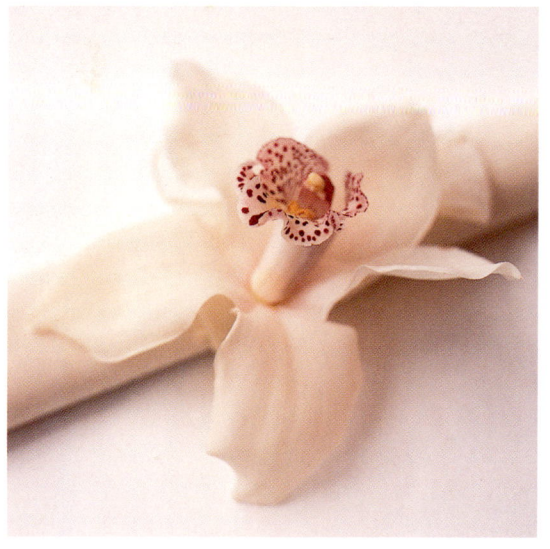

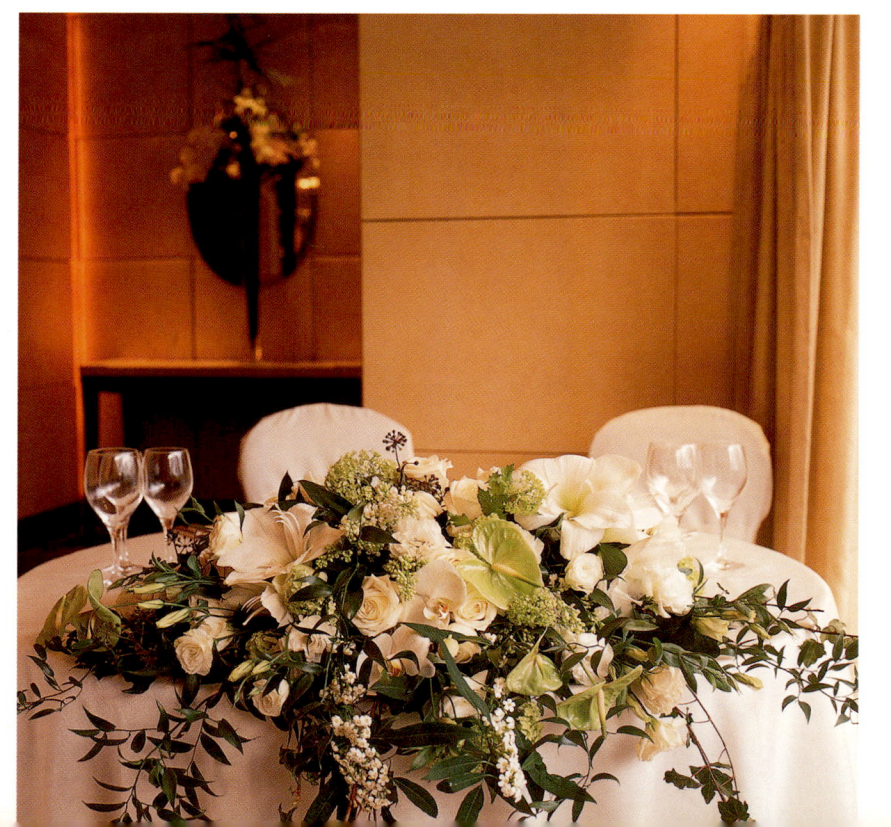

"It could not have been more perfect and magical." KEREN

OPPOSITE (CLOCKWISE FROM TOP LEFT) Open amaryllis (*Hippeastrum* 'Mont Blanc') are tied together at the base of their flower heads to create a living topiary; A tall flared vase is lined with snake grass (equisetum) and filled with cymbidium orchids and blossom; Low, trailing table arrangements are perfect for top tables as they create a lovely frame for photographs; A delicate cymbidium orchid is tucked into each guest's napkin. THIS PAGE, ABOVE The two heights of table arrangements – amaryllis trees and taller glass flutes filled with phalaenopsis orchids. LEFT A sushi bar is decorated with a large glass vase filled with Brussels sprouts and savoy cabbages and topped with roses, cabbages and cymbidium orchids. BELOW A perspex dish has been filled with a big glass globe, bunches of pussy willow and two large balls of amaryllis.

table settings

However large or small your wedding you will require some decoration on the tables. This can be as simple as a lovely plant, such as a Marguerite daisy, with its pot wrapped in muslin or a seasonal chrysanthemum in a basket. For a slightly higher budget you can choose a simple tied bunch of seasonal flowers such as daffodils or tulips in spring, cornflowers in summer, dahlias or zinnias for autumn or berries and foliage for winter.

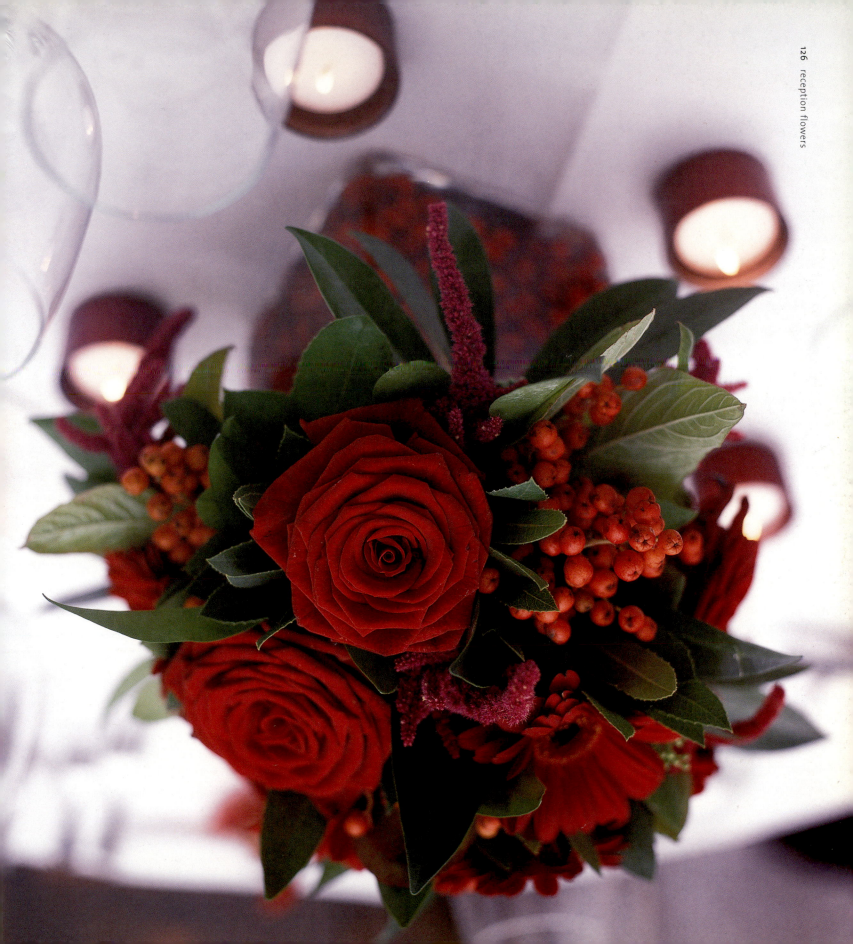

OPPOSITE Cube vases are the most versatile vase for table decorations. Filled with cranberries and topped with 'Grand Prix' roses, red cotoneaster berries, gerbera 'Chateau', dark red amaranthus and skimmia, this monochromatic table centre is perfect for an autumn wedding. **THIS PAGE** By folding the napkin you can create a pocket – the perfect place to arrange an orchid head, such as this cymbidium orchid. In autumn, small apples and pears that do not make the grade for human consumption are waxed and covered in glitter for decoration.

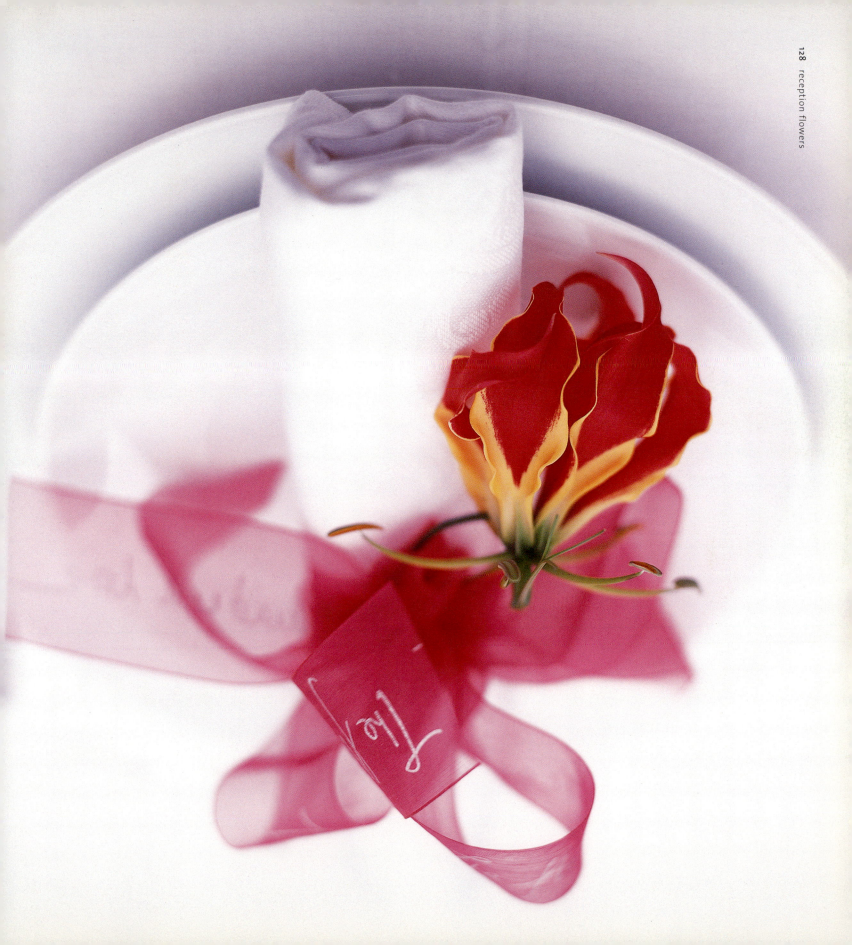

OPPOSITE A gloriosa lily has been tied with a mousseline bow to a napkin. The inscription on the ribbon is 'The flower is a leaf mad with love' by the German philosopher Goethe. THIS PAGE Three yellow ranunculus (my favourite flower) have been tied with raffia for a simple but striking napkin decoration.

cakes

One of the highlights of the reception is, of course, the cutting of the cake. There are so many imaginative cake makers available that you really can have anything you desire from a multi-tiered selection of small cup cakes to a lavish five-tiered sugar-flowered design. The choice of flowers to decorate the cake is equally wide and, once you've agreed on a design, your florist will be able to advise you on the perfect floral embellishments.

OPPOSITE (CLOCKWISE FROM FAR LEFT) A pink-striped stacked cake has been decorated at the base with a ring of pink roses 'Rosita Vendella', 'Dolce Vita', 'Barbie' and pink hydrangeas; Individual cakes have been simply decorated with a marguerite daisy; A highly decorative cake with floral embroidery icing has been topped with a small trailing arrangement of pink and purple flowers to match. They are sweet peas (*Lathyrus odoratus*), lysimachia, ranunculus, love-in-a-mist (nigella), *Leucocoryne* 'Caravelle' and trailing ivies THIS PAGE A three-tiered square cake has been decorated with two tiers of multi-coloured roses (the bright orange 'Narangar', the burgundy bi-colour 'Ruby Red', the bright pink 'Milano', the golden 'Tresor 2000' and the burgundy 'Black Baccara') and a top box filled with lines of roses.

a touch of the romantic

just seven months after meeting her at a private gallery, Viorel visited Natalia in Barcelona and he proposed with a gorgeous classic ring from Tiffany. Natalia, originally from Russia, and Viorel, from Romania, wanted their respective backgrounds to be reflected in their wedding, and so began to plan a wedding with lots of traditional touches from their homelands. Natalia loved Tchaikovsky's *Swan Lake* and so that became the theme for their very romantic wedding. A mint-green feather was slipped into each of the wedding invitations and ostrich-feather boas were used to decorate the flower arrangements. Her bridesmaid also wore mint green and Viorel sported a mint-green cravat. Natalia chose to hold white calla lilies with an ostrich-feather collar, which looked amazing with her fairy-tale gown. After their civil ceremony at a register office, the happy couple released a pair of white love doves, which is a gesture of peace and love to celebrate the vows the couple had just exchanged. The doves flew away together, symbolising the new union (and continuing on Natalia's romantic bird theme). As most of their guests were visiting from overseas, Natalia and Viorel wanted to show their guests a little bit of the city and so they hired traditional buses to take them all to a huge Ferris wheel on the banks of a river, on which they had hired two private capsules for the wedding party. Here they all enjoyed champagne while admiring the panorama of the city below them.

The reception was held at Natalia's favourite venue, a minimalist hotel – a large white space with the entrance filled with masses of white phalaenopsis orchids. At first, the guests mingled in the gardens while sipping more champagne and listening to Tchaikovsky's *Swan Lake* played by a string quartet. They could also admire two huge ice sculptures of swans decorated with dendrobium orchids, pink calla lilies and long ruscus garlands that had been set into a square pond in the centre of the garden. We had also decorated all the other ponds with floating orchid heads and the iron arch over the gate that marked the entrance to the garden with white bougainvillea, pale pink phalaenopsis orchids and green trailing amaranthus. Following drinks and Russian caviar in the hotel grounds the guests went into the restaurant for dinner. Here the black tablecloths were decorated with square vases filled with limes and white 'Iceberg' roses and encircled with white ostrich feathers. The minimalist interior of the hotel was the perfect backdrop for the bold contemporary theme. Each name tag was attached to a single pink calla lily with a stem of bear grass. After the dinner, the couple cut their swan-like white chocolate cake while a Russian gypsy band played. Following their first dance (a Russian waltz), the dancing began with a mixture of Russian and Romanian tunes, giving the reception a real Eastern-European theme.

ABOVE Natalia and Viorel share a romantic moment outside the register office. Viorel's arum lily buttonhole matches Natalia's bridal bouquet. His buttonhole was trimmed with bear grass which also encircled the bridesmaids' bouquets and was used to tie the place-names on to calla lilies for the reception.

RIGHT Natalia chose to decorate an arch in the garden at the hotel where her guests were to enjoy Russian caviar and champagne. The flowers include white bougainvillea, pale pink phalaenopsis orchids and green trailing amaranthus. **BELOW LEFT** The hotel interior was very minimalist and so Natalia chose structured table arrangements of domes of roses placed in glass cubes lined with limes. Each guest was given a pink calla lily to which their name tag had been tied with bear grass. **BELOW RIGHT** Natalia's *Swan Lake* theme was highlighted in the garden where two ice swan sculptures were floated on the central pond and surrounded by orchid heads. The guests mingled outside while listening to Tchaikovsky's *Swan Lake*.

"The pale colours and the feathers added the air of a romantic fairytale – just the way I imagined my wedding!" NATALIA

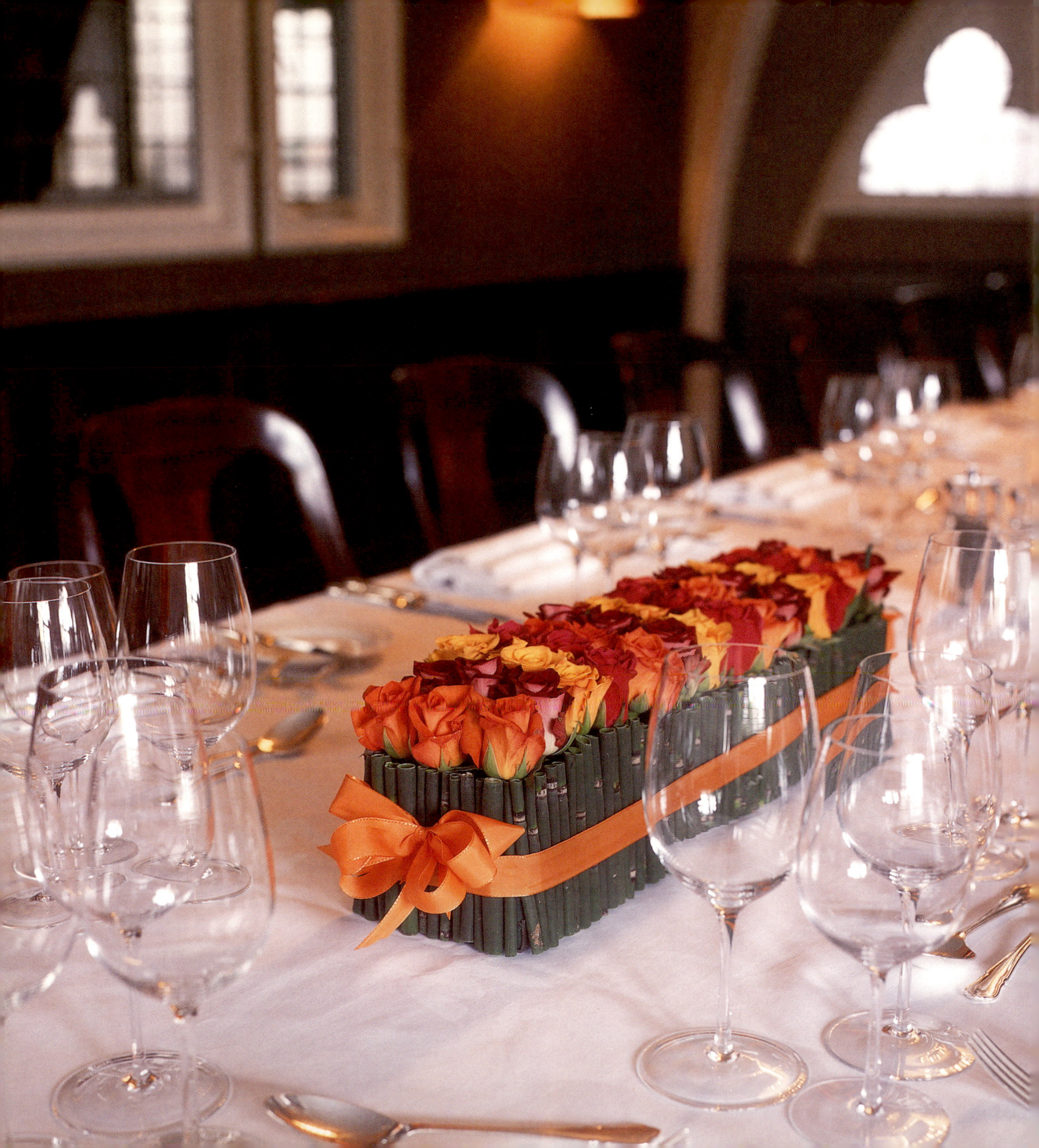

how to make a centrepiece arrangement

Long tables require linear arrangements for their centres. They can often be very narrow (some are only 60-cm wide) which means that once you have got place settings on either side of the table you have very little room for any decoration. The arrangement shown here was originally designed for a long narrow table because it is a neat structural design and suits a narrow space perfectly. This arrangement is the width of a standard block of floral foam, called a rackette. It has a plastic base – perfect for tables. To edge the plastic and the foam you can use equisetum as seen here or any other type of reed. Lavender or rosemary pinned all around the foam would work equally well or another favourite of mine is to use cinnamon sticks for winter weddings.

The choice of flower is more limited than the choice of plant material for the surround as, for this design to look sculptural, it needs to include flower heads of a uniform size. Even if you use roses as I have done you need to make sure that the heads are of a similar size to create the uniform bands of colour. Small germini gerberas would work well or try dahlias or zinnias. Choose vibrant colours – practically any combinations work as long as you make sure that each variety of rose has the same depth of colour. (Pastels can also work, with the use of white.) I like to take a combination and place colours that contrast with one another to make the linear arrangement more striking.

MATERIALS

50-cm rackette of floral foam
A selection of long heavy stub wires
3 bunches of equisetum
52 stems of roses in at least five different colours
A length of matching ribbon
Scissors

STEP BY STEP

1 Soak the block of foam in water until the air bubbles stop rising. Bend the stub wires into two and then cut the long stems into three or four lengths, depending on the height, so that the equisetum will be about 2.5 cm above the edge of the floral foam.
2 Pin the equisetum into the foam and work all the way round the block. Take care to pin the reeds in at the same height, so that this can later be concealed by the ribbon.
3 Cut a length of ribbon so that it will fit around all four sides and tie it at one end of the block. Take another piece of ribbon and make three loops to create a bow at one end.
4 Cut the rose heads down to about 5 cm of stem, so that their heads sit just above the edge of the equisetum and there is enough stem to take up water from the soaked foam. For the design to work, it is important that the lines of colour are even. Think carefully about the order of the bands of colour that will look the most striking. I like to use a dark colour next to a light or bright colour to create the most impact. Add the roses and mist with a water spray.

how to make an **orange basket**

Using fruit and vegetables is an inexpensive way to add more natural texture and colour to your arrangements. Fruit also adds a very fresh look to arrangements and is perfect for a table centre for a special occasion. I am drawn to fruit and vegetable markets for inspiration for my arrangements from the appearance of the soft fruits (such as red currants, strawberries and raspberries) in early summer to the less productive winter months when I may be on the look out for vibrant citrus fruits to add colour. This arrangement was initially conceived with apples and you can see an autumnal version of this on page 108. Any hard fruit such as citrus fruits or apples can be wired into a basket. You need a sturdy loose-weave basket to make the base and heavy stub wires to push through the centre of the fruit and attach them to the basket. I prefer baskets with chicken wire in them, which makes it easier, but you can use any basket as long as there is room to push the wires through. For taller baskets I have also used vegetables. Leeks are one of my favourites; I love the root structure and the graduation of colour from white to green. Turnips and heather were used for weddings with a Scottish theme and pomegranates filled with garden roses also worked extraordinarily well. You are limited only by your imagination so choose seasonal vegetables or fruit that can give great impact for a reasonable price. For this arrangement I wanted to create a vibrant clash of colour to complement the intense orange. fruit.

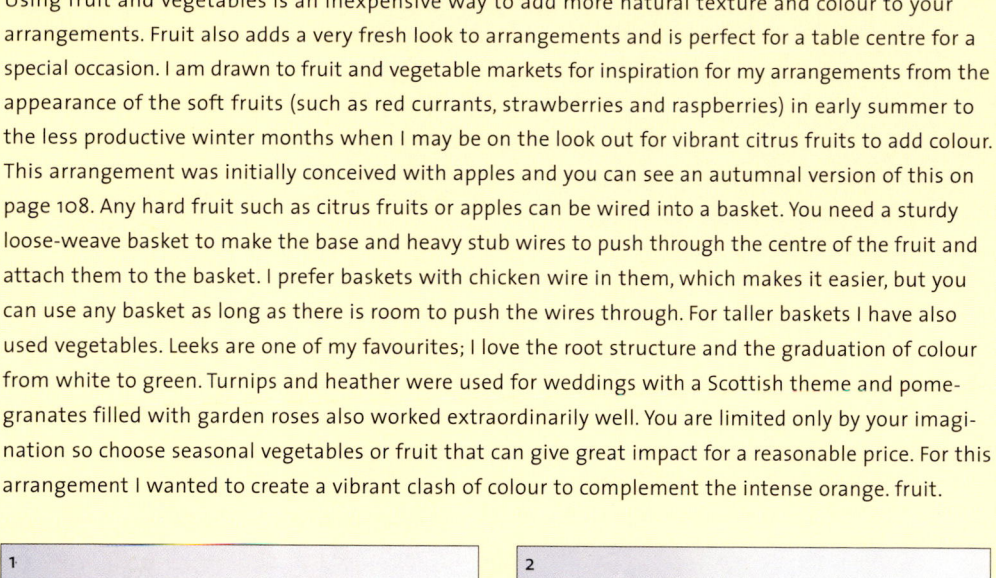

MATERIALS

24 to 30 pieces of fruit
1 block of floral foam and a sturdy basket
A couple of handfuls of moss
Scissors and a selection of long strong stub wires
10 'Queensday' roses
10 stems of Icelandic poppies
10 stems of 'Pauline Burgundy' ranunculus
5 stems of *Viburnum opulus* and gardenia foliage
10 stems of huckleberry foliage
5 stems of long gloriosa lilies
7 stems of 'Milano' roses

STEP BY STEP

1 Wire the fruit by placing a long heavy wire through the centre and then bring the two ends together underneath and twist. If it is strong enough you will be able to hold the fruit upright on the wires. If it bends use two wires together.

2 Wire the fruit onto the basket, completing the lower ring first. Line it with moss. Add a plastic pot filled with soaked floral foam. The foam should be 5 cm above the top of the wired fruit.

3 Using the three foliage plants, first create the round shape of the arrangement, making sure that some of the *Viburnum opulus* falls over the edge of the basket.

4 Arrange the 'Queensday' roses at different heights and depths throughout the arrangement (but all radiating from the centre). Next add the poppies after re-sealing the ends of their stems with a lit candle. Finally gently guide the stems of rancunulus and gloriosa into the foam.

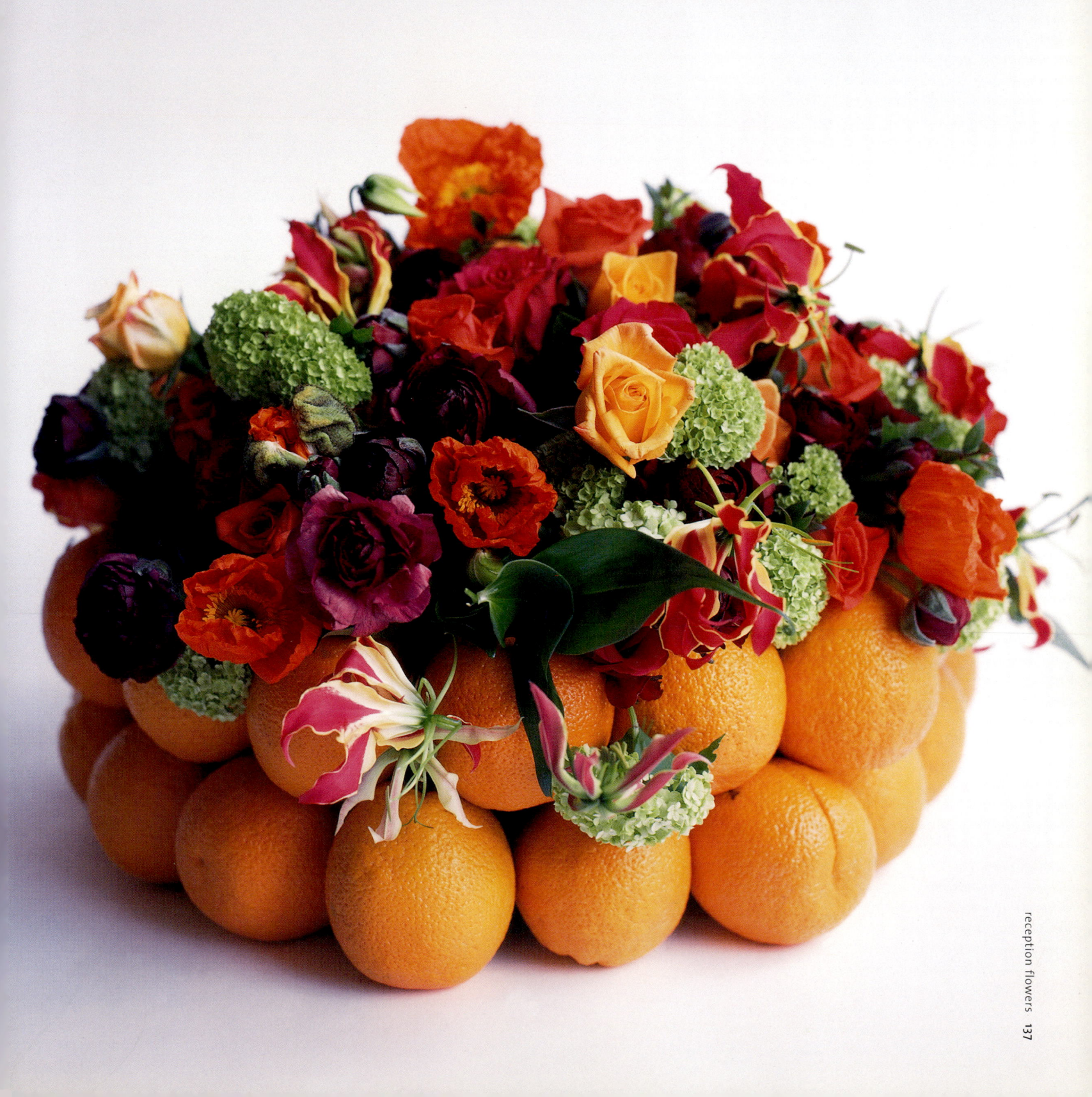

elegance personified

the historic setting of Syon Park, a magnificent eighteenth-century house, was the choice of wedding venue for Anna and Philipp, who met while working at an investment bank. Although Philipp is from Germany and Anna from the Midlands they wanted to marry in the city where they first met. The classic wedding ceremony took place in the house itself while the reception was held in the truly stunning Great Conservatory – I have to admit it is one of my favourite wedding venues.

After an initial visit to my studio, Anna, Philipp and their baby daughter Sophie met me at Syon to look at the location and decide on the decorations. They chose a pale cream and white theme with a touch of pink and decided to include some sweet peas and tuberose for scent, and silver eucalyptus to match the hired chairs and urns. Anna and Philipp especially wanted the celebration to be perfumed so that the wonderful fragrance would always remind them of the day. The couple chose to have low arrangements for their tables in the conservatory as the party was quite intimate with only 80 guests and the venue is relatively small. For the ceremony itself, Anna and Philipp chose to have two large pedestals filled with matching blooms and to line the aisle with pew ends. After the ceremony everything had to be cleared from Syon House as the family are still in residence and so we positioned ten of the pew ends as chairbacks around the top table and also moved the large pedestal displays to the conservatory. This was all completed discreetly while the guests enjoyed drinks and canapés in the beautiful gardens, and the informal photography was going on. Anna included some lovely personal touches to her reception by giving everyone pots of bubble blowers, which were used instead of confetti as the couple entered the reception. They also ordered a traditional bus to transport all their guests to Syon Park and chose a white cab decorated with white ribbons for themselves.

ABOVE Anna and Philipp stride out together in the library of Syon House after their ceremony, in the pink with their 'Bianca Candy' roses. Anna wore a silk organza dress beaded with Swarovski crystals and a matching tiara. Philipp's grey morning suit, tie and waistcoat co-ordinate beautifully with the bridesmaids' silver silk dresses. **OPPOSITE** Two large pedestals of matching blooms are the focal point of the arrangements at the ceremony.

For the ceremony Anna had chosen silver chairs to continue her silver colour scheme and and so we decided to use silver vases and plinths. As it turned out the silver chairs did not make it to the ceremony (although they did arrive in time for the reception) and so we used the ones at Syon. I mention this as to their absolute credit Anna and Philipp did not let this incident spoil their special day. Often when you have been planning an event for a long time and have taken time to decide on all the details and hire lots of extras to ensure that absolutely everything co-ordinates it can be very upsetting if things do not work exactly as planned. However it is essential to remember that it is your special day and nothing should stop you enjoying it!

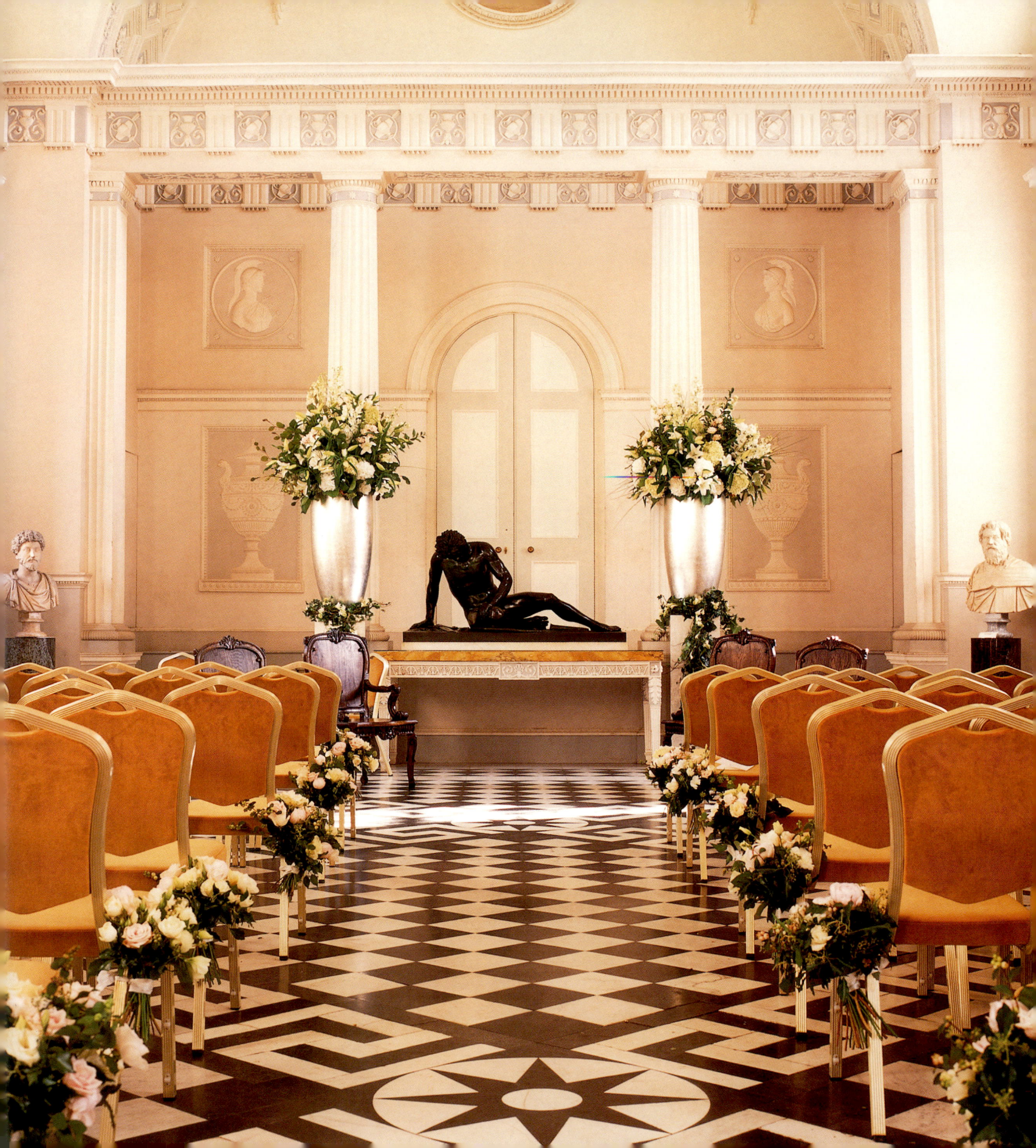

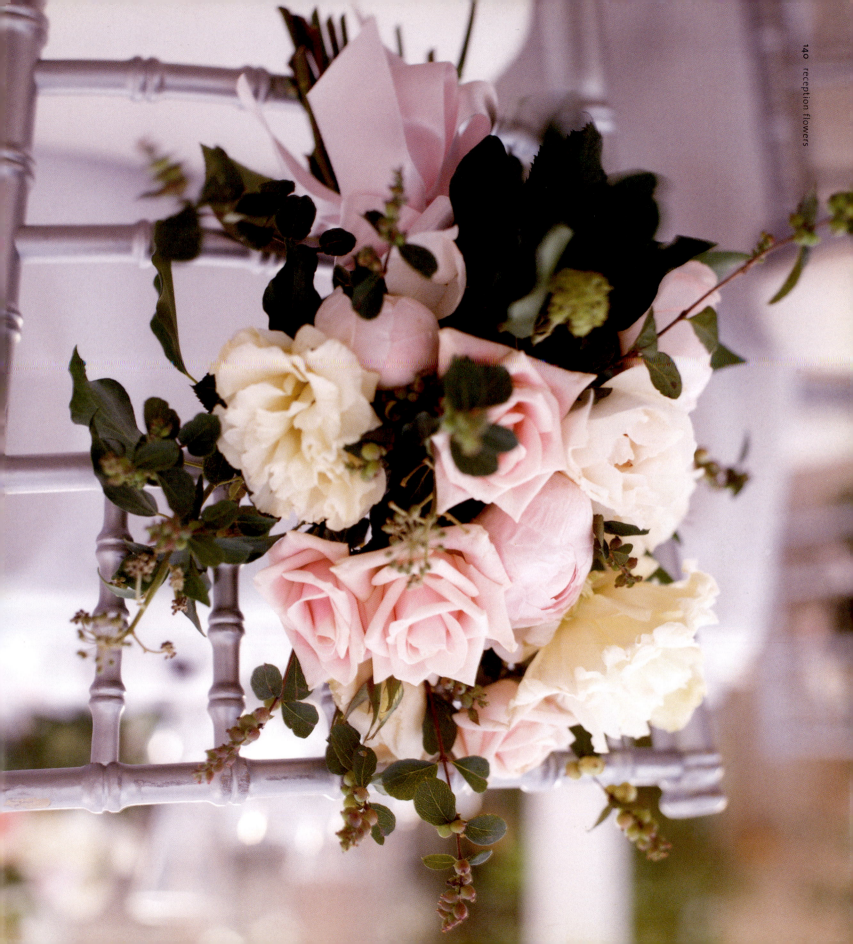

OPPOSITE This is a classic chairback made for the top table, created by tying summer flowers and foliage into a simple swag. The peony roses are 'Scented Pink' and the classic open rose is 'Bianca Candy', which is mixed with silver *Eucalyptus* 'Baby Blue', to tone with the chair colour, and pale pink snow-berries (*Symphoricarpos* x *doorenbosii* 'Red Pearl'), to blend with the roses. **ABOVE LEFT** A bridegroom often has a different colour but-tonhole from those of the ushers to match the bride's bouquet, so our groom wore a pale pink 'Bianca Candy' rose trimmed with snowberries and edged with camellia leaves. The cream 'Vendela' is one of the most popu-lar wedding roses because of its delicate colour and perfect bud shape. **ABOVE RIGHT** The bridesmaids carry simple tied bouquets of 'Vendela' roses edged with camellia leaves. **LEFT** A glass bowl is a classic container for any location. The roses have been mixed with fragrant tuberose and I used white lysimachia and cream lisianthus as they are long and droopy, creating some movement. In the background is a huge pedestal of flowers that tones with the table arrangements.

"The conservatory was more lovely and magical than anything I could ever have imagined. I loved my bouquet above anything. It was perfect and exquisite – and I had serious second thoughts about tossing it because I would have liked to keep it forever!" ANNA

LEFT A stacked American cake by the Little Venice Cake Company set on a silver cake stand edged with fragrant stephanotis, rose petals and votives. The cake included a few sparkly iced crystals to match Anna's shoes, dress and tiara. ABOVE One of the grooms-men in front of the conservatory at Syon sporting a champagne 'Vendela' rose button-hole. OPPOSITE, TOP LEFT The name cards were laid out on scented garden rose petals. OPPOSITE, TOP RIGHT Anna chose 'Bianca Candy' roses for her bouquet to match her dress. They were wired into a delicate posy with a ribboned handle and Philipp sported a matching buttonhole. OPPOSITE, BOTTOM RIGHT A tied posy of 'Vendela and 'Bianca Candy' roses with white sweet peas and lysimachia, edged with camellias and snow-berries. OPPOSITE, BOTTOM LEFT Standard ligustrum trees decorated with ribbons and roses are placed at either side of the conservatory doors to welcome guests.

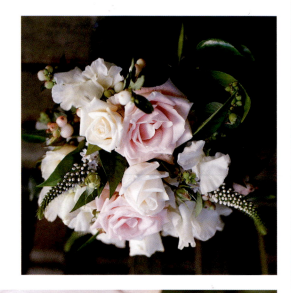

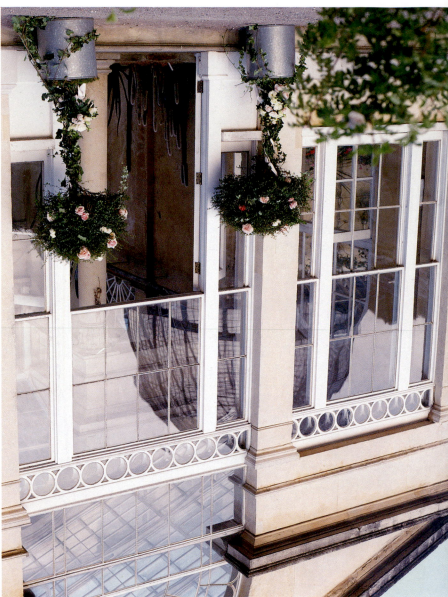

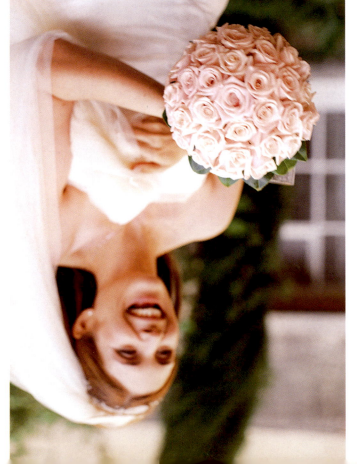

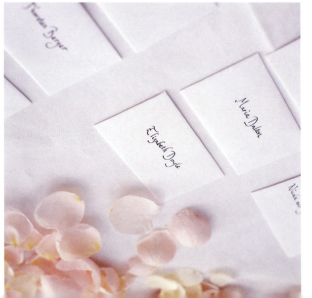

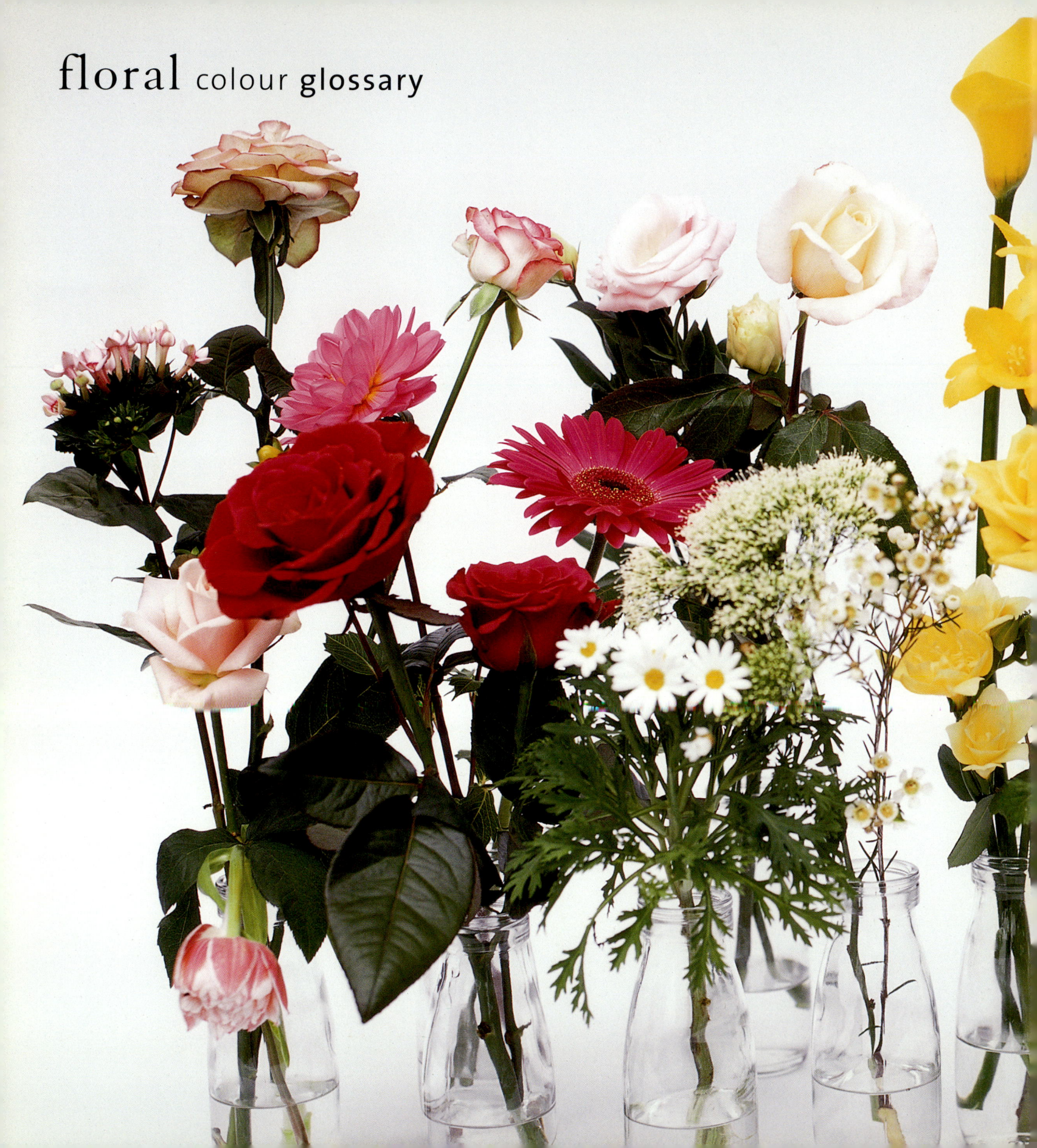

floral colour glossary

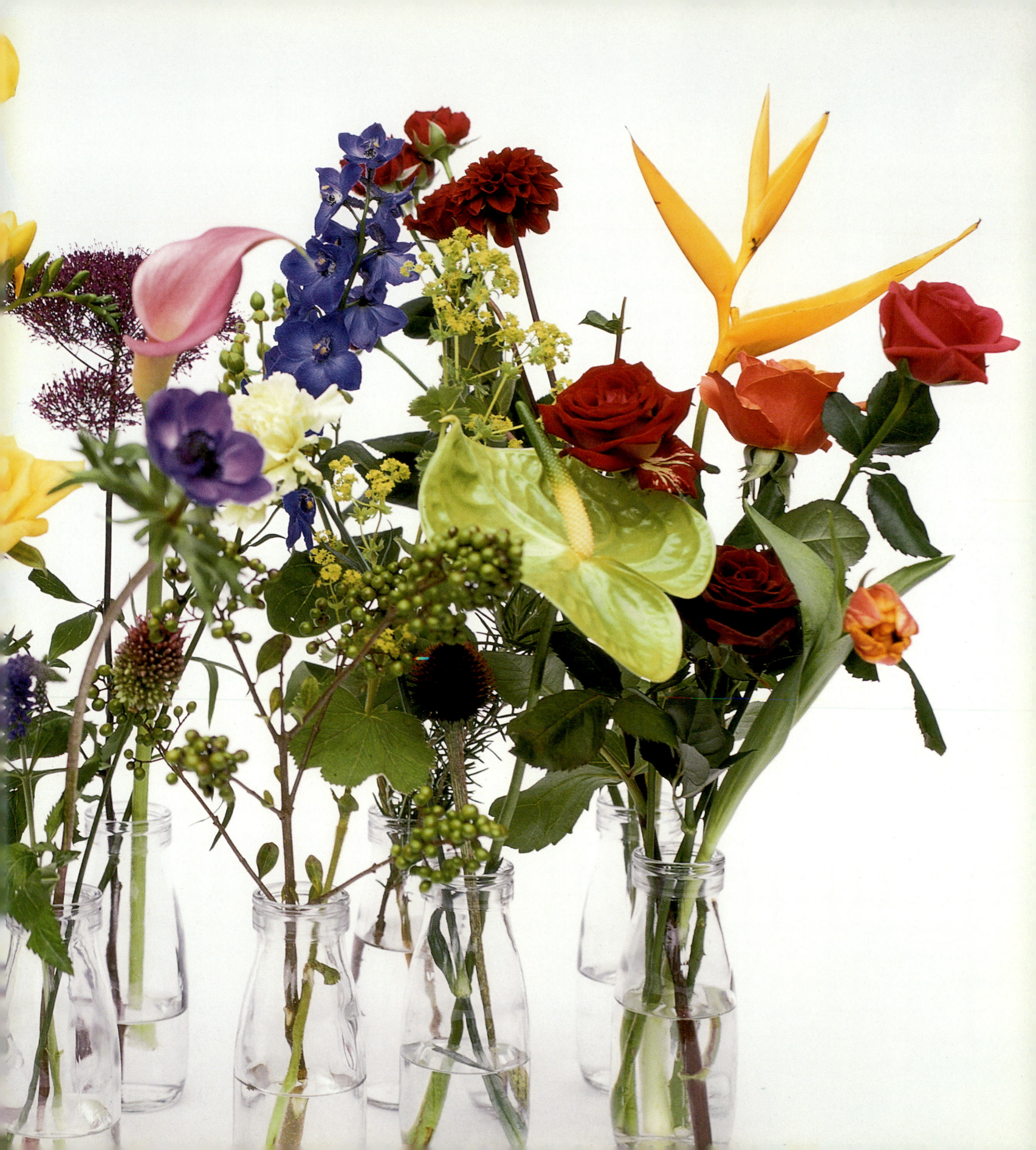

1 *Mimosa* 'Yellow Island' 2 *Pittosporum crassifolium* 'Variegatum' 3 *Helleborus argutifolius* 4 *Lysimachia clethroides* (white loosestrife) 5 *Genista tenera* 'Golden Shower' (broom) 6 *Tulipa* 'Weber's Parrot' 7 *Ranunculus* 'Ranobelle Donkergeel' 8 *Euphorbia fulgens* 'Quicksilver' 9 *Narcissus* 'Cheerfulness' 10 *Narcissus* 'Golden Ducat' 11 *Lathyrus odoratus* (sweet pea) 12 *Populus deltoides* (eastern cottonwood) 13 *Polianthes tuberosa* (tuberose) 14 *Euonymus fortunei* 'Emerald'n'Gold' 15 *Tulipa* 'Monte Carlo' 16 *Zantedeschia* 'Florex Gold' (arum lily, calla lily) 17 *Rosa* 'Taxi' 18 *Spiraea nipponica* 'Snowmound' 19 *Antirrhinum majus* 'Winter Euro Yellow' (snapdragon) 20 *Gerbera germini* 'Kaliki' 21 *Viburnum opulus* (guelder rose) 22 *Abutilon vitifolium* var. *album* 23 *Eustoma grandiflorum* 'Piccolo Yellow' (lisianthus) 24 *Polygonatum* (Solomon's seal) 25 *Forsythia* x *intermedia* 26 *Prunus glandulosa* 'Albo Plena'

1 *Eucalyptus ficifolia* 2 *Rosa* 'Aqua' 3 *Camellia* x *williamsii* 'E.G. Waterhouse' 4 *Rosa* 'Milano' 5 *Anemone coronaria* 'Mona Lisa Pink' 6 *Tulipa* 'Upstar' 7 *Lathyrus odoratus* (sweet pea) 8 *Tulipa* 'Lucky Strike' 9 *Hyacinthus orientalis* 'Anna Marie' (hyacinth) 10 *Paeonia* 'Sarah Bernhardt' 11 *Paeonia* 'Bowl of Beauty' 12 *Eustoma grandiflorum* 'Moon Pink' (lisianthus) 13 *Chamelaucium uncinatum* 'Wendy Rose' (Geralton wax) 14 *Phlox* 'Bright Eyes' 15 *Rosa* 'Laminuette' 16 *Tulipa* 'Salmon Parrot' 17 *Gerbera germini* 'Sonate' 18 *Chaenomeles japonica* (flowering quince) 19 *Gladiolus* 'Priscilla' 20 *Prunus serrulata* 21 *Ranunculus* 'Ranobelle Inra dark pink' 22 *Ranunculus* 'Ranobelle Inra light pink' 23 *Antirrhinum majus* 'Potomac Red' (snapdragon)

1 *Delphinium* 'Skyline' **2** *Agapanthus* 'Donau' **3** *Consolida ajacis* 'Sydney Purple' (larkspur) **4** *Delphinium* Belladonna Group 'Völkerfrieden' **5** *Liatris spicata* 'Blue Bird' (gayfeather) **6** *Veronica longifolia* 'Blauriesen' **7** *Delphinium* Belladonna Group 'Sky Lady' **8** *Freesia* 'Côte d'Azur' **9** *Matthiola incana* 'Arabella' (stock) **10** *Tulipa* 'Black Parrot' **11** *Iris* 'Purple Rain' **12** *Lathyrus odoratus* (sweet pea) **13** *Aquilegia* 'Blue Lady' (columbine) **14** *Scilla siberica* (Siberian squill) **15** *Myosotis sylvatica* (forget-me-not) **16** *Hyacinthus orientalis* 'Delft Blue' (hyacinth) **17** *Muscari armeniacum* 'Blue Dream' (grape hyancinth) **18** *Anemone coronaria* 'Galil Purper' **19** *Anemone coronaria* 'Marianne Blue' **20** *Matthiola incana* 'Lucinda Purple' (stock) **21** *Syringa* x *hyacinthiflora* 'Esther Staley' (lilac) **22** *Trachelium caeruleum* 'Blue Wonder' (blue throatwort) **23** *Syringa vulgaris* 'Andenken an Ludwig Spaeth' (lilac)

1 *Viburnum opulus* (guelder rose) 2 *Dahlia* 'Bicolour Karma' 3 *Rosa* 'Extase' 4 *Rosa* 'Jacaranda' 5 *Dianthus barbatus* 'Monarch Series' (sweet William) 6 *Gerbera* 'Dark Serena' 7 *Cirsium japonicum* 'Pink Beauty' 8 *Celosia argentea* var. *cristata* Cristata Group 'Bombay Pink' (cockscomb) 9 *Moluccella laevis* (bells of Ireland) 10 *Consolida ajacis* 'Sydney Rose' (larkspur) 11 *Paeonia lactiflora* 'Karl Rosenfield' 12 *Sorbus aria* 'Lutescens' (whitebeam) 13 *Lathyrus odoratus* (sweetpea) 14 *Rosa* 'Milano' 15 *Astilbe* x *arendsii* 'Erika' 16 *Eustoma grandiflorum* 'Mariachi Pink' (lisianthus) 17 *Rosa* 'Saint Celia' 18 *Crataegus laevigata* 'Paul's Scarlet' (may, hawthorn) 19 *Protea nerifolia* 20 *Lilium* 'Red Sox' 21 *Celosia argentea* var. *cristata* Plumosa Group 'Bombay Fire'

1 *Physalis alkekengi* (Chinese lantern)   2 *Populus deltoides* (eastern cottonwood)   3 *Crocosmia* 'Lucifer' (montbretia)
4 *Chrysanthemum* 'Salmon Fairie'   5 *Leucospermum reflexum* 'Lutea' (pincushion)   6 *Helenium* 'Moerheim Beauty'   7 *Zantedeschia*
'Florex Gold' (arum lily, calla lily)   8 *Capsicum annuum*   9 *Carthamus tinctorius* 'Kinko' (safflower, false saffron)   10 *Anethum
graveolens* (dill)   11 *Hydrangea macrophylla*   12 *Rosa* 'Golden Gate'   13 *Helianthus annuus* 'Sonja' (sunflower)   14 *Hypericum* 'Jade
Flair' (St. John's Wort)   15 *Chrysanthemum* 'Shamrock'   16 *Sandersonia aurantiaca*   17 *Malus* x *robusta* 'Red Sentinel' (crab apple)

1 *Gentiana* 'Sky' (gentian) 2 *Delphinium* Belladonna Group 'Blue Shadow' 3 *Rosa* 'Blue Moon' 4 *Ageratum houstonianum* 'Blue Horizon' 5 *Centaurea montana* (knapweed) 6 *Scabiosa stellata* 'Ping Pong' (pincushion flower, scabious) 7 *Lathyrus odoratus* 'Lila' (sweet pea) 8 *Cotinus coggygria* 'Royal Purple' (smoke bush) 9 *Zantedeschia* 'Anneke' (arum lily, calla lily) 10 *Delphinium* 'Faust' 11 *Allium sphaerocephalon* 12 *Delphinium* 'Lilac Arrow' 13 *Hydrangea macrophylla* 'Blue' 14 *Scabiosa caucasica* 'Clive Greaves' (pincushion flower, scabious) 15 *Rosa* 'Blue Gene' 16 *Delphinium* 'Skyline'

1 *Symphoricarpos* **x** *doorenbosii* 'White Hedge' (snowberry)   **2** *Astilbe* 'America'   **3** *Symphoricarpos* 'Pink Pearl' (snowberry)
4 *Panicum miliaceum* (millet)   **5** *Gerbera germini* 'Leila'   **6** *Bouvardia* 'Bridesmaid'   **7** *Rosa* 'Jacaranda'   **8** *Rosa* 'Aqua'   **9** *Rosa*
'Duo Unique'   **10** *Sedum telephium* 'Mohrchen'   **11** *Cirsium japonicum* 'Pink Beauty'   **12** *Rosa* 'Mimi Eden'   **13** *Rosa* 'Illusion'
14 *Celosia argentea* var. *cristata* Cristata Group 'Bombay Rose'   **15** *Alchemilla mollis* (lady's mantle)   **16** *Dahlia* 'Karma Thalia'
17 *Zantedeschia* 'Fantail Candy' (arum lily, calla lily)

1 *Rosa* 'Bianca' 2 *Lathyrus odoratus* (sweet pea) 3 *Celosia argentea* var. *cristata* Cristata Group 'Bombay Green' (cockscomb)
4 *Dahlia* 'Canberra' 5 *Dianthus* 'Prado' (pink) 6 *Gypsophila* 'Million Stars' 7 *Lysimachia clethroides* 'Helene' (loosestrife)
8 *Trachelium caeruleum* 'Album' (throatwort) 9 *Rosa virginiana* 10 *Scabiosa caucasica* 'Hermina' (pincushion flower, scabious)
11 *Anthemis tinctoria* (golden marguerite, oxeye chamomile) 12 *Symphoricarpos albus* 'White Pearl' (snowberry)

1 *Ilex aquifolium* 'Golden Verboon' (common holly) **2** *Solanum integrifolium* (tomato eggplant) **3** *Fagus sylvatica* (beech)
4 *Leucospermum cordifolium* 'Tango' (pincushion) **5** *Dendrobium* 'Tang' **6** *Ranunculus* 'Ranobelle Inra Oranjerood'
7 *Quercus robur* (English oak, common oak) **8** *Zantedeschia* 'Treasure' (arum lily, calla lily) **9** *Eucalyptus pulverulenta*
10 *Rosa* 'Macarena' **11** *Chrysanthemum* 'Reagan Orange' **12** *Euphorbia fulgens* 'Beatrix' **13** *Gladiolus* 'Esta Bonita'
14 *Chrysanthemum* 'Tom Pearce' **15** *Hippeastrum* 'Rilona' (amaryllis) **16** *Quercus palustris* (pin oak) **17** *Tulipa* 'Prinses Irene'

1 *Gladiolus* 'Addi' 2 *Capsicum annum* (pepper) 3 *Anemone* 'Mona Lisa Red' 4 *Rosa canina* (dog rose, common brier)
5 *Hippeastrum* 'Red Lion' (amaryllis) 6 *Photinia* x *fraseri* 'Red Robin' 7 *Ilex verticillata* 'Oosterwijk' (winterberry)
8 *Gerbera germini* 'Salsa' 9 *Rosa* 'Grand Prix' 10 *Callistemon citrinus* (crimson bottlebrush) 11 *Chrysanthemum* 'Reagan
Red' 12 *Skimmia japonica* 'Rubella' 13 *Leucadendron* 'Safari Sunset' 14 *Chrysanthemum* 'Early Bird Red' 15 *Tulipa*
'Prominence' 16 *Anthurium* 'Choco' (flamingo flower) 17 *Rosa* 'Black Baccara' 18 *Ranunculus* 'Pauline Scarlet'
19 *Gerbera germini* 'Midnight' 20 *Alpinia purpurata* (red ginger)

1 *Hippeastrum* 'Ludwig Dazzler' (amaryllis) 2 *Euphorbia fulgens* 'Largo White' 3 *Rosa* 'Avalanche' 4 *Brassica oleracea* 'Corgy White' (ornamental cabbage) 5 *Chamelaucium uncinatum* 'Blondie' (Geraldton wax) 6 *Lilium longiflorum* 'White Europe' (Easter lily) 7 *Brunia albiflora* 8 *Dahlia* 'Karma Serena' 9 *Gladiolus* 'Mont Blanc' 10 *Gossypium herbaceum* (levant cotton) 11 *Genista* 12 *Eucharis amazonica* 13 *Syringa vulgaris* 'Primrose' (lilac) 14 *Hyacinthus orientalis* 'Mont Blanc' (hyacinth) 15 *Ranunculus* 'Ranobelle Inra White' 16 *Narcissus tazetta* 'Ziva' 17 *Lilum* 'Casa Blanca' 18 *Phalaenopsis* 'Alpha' 19 *Gypsophila* 'Lucky Stars' 20 *Hydrangea arborescens* 'Annabelle' 21 *Anthurium* 'Bianca'

1 *Zantedeschia aethiopica* 'Colombe de la Paix' (arum lily, calla lily) 2 *Eucharis amazonica* 3 *Brachyglottis* 'Sunshine' (senecio) 4 *Aster novi-belgii* 'M. C. Snowy' (Michaelmas daisy) 5 *Chrysanthemum* 'Reagan White' 6 *Eustoma grandiflorum* 'Alice White' (lisianthus) 7 *Freesia* 'Alaska' 8 *Ornithogalum thyrsoides* 'Mount Fuji' (chincherinchee) 9 *Hypericum androsaemum* 'King Flair' (tutsan) 10 *Rosmarinus officinalis* (rosemary) 11 *Dendrobium* 'Madame Pompadour White' 12 *Rosa* 'Iceberg' 13 *Rosa* 'Akito' 14 *Gerbera jamesonii* 'Bianca' (Barbarton daisy) 15 *Lilium longiflorum* 'Snow Queen' (Easter lily) 16 *Stephanotis floribunda* (bridal wreath, Madagascar jasmine) 17 *Cymbidium* 'R. B. Mieke' 18 *Anthurium* 'Captain' 19 *Dianthus* 'Dover' (carnation) 20 *Gypsophila* 'Little White'

index

page numbers in *italic* refer to the illustrations

A

Abutilon vitifolium var. *album* 146
achillea *101*
Agapanthus 99
  'Donau' *148*
Ageratum houstonianum 'Blue Horizon' *151*
Alchemilla 14, 109
  mollis 20, 44, *152*
alder berries 74
Allium sphaerocephalon *151*
alpinia gingers *39*, *97*, 155
amaranthus 11, 14, *97*, 110, 111, 113, *126*, *133*
amaryllis see *Hippeastrum*
Anemone 18
  'Galil Purper' *148*
  'Marianne Blue' *148*
  'Mona Lisa Pink' *147*
  'Mona Lisa Red' *155*
Anthemis tinctoria *153*
Anthurium 38, 48, 98
  'Bianca' *156*
  'Captain' *157*
  'Choco' *155*
  'Midori' *10*, *40*, *41*, *57*, *92*, 121
Antirrhinum 20
  majus 'Potomac Red' *147*
  majus 'Winter Euro Yellow' *146*
apples *108*, *127*
Aquilegia 'Blue Lady' *148*
arum lilies 48, 80, 98, 118, *132*, *146*, 150, 151, 152, 154, 157
Asclepias physocarpa *109*
aspidistra leaves 47, *92*, 92, 98, *125*
Aster novi-belgii 'M.C. Snowy' *157*
Astilbe
  'America' *152*
  x *arendsii* 'Erika' *53*, 149
astrantia 8
autumn flowers 20, 32–5, 152–4

B

bag corsages *19*, 69
bamboo 98
baskets *8*, 67, 68, *136–7*
bay 34
bear grass *132*, 132, *133*
bells of Ireland see *Molucella laevis*
blossom 18, *122*
blue flowers *148*, *151*
bougainvillea 14, *133*
bouquets 9, 42–63
Bouvardia 'Bridesmaid' *152*
box 8
bracelets 67
Brachyglottis 'Sunshine' *157*
bridesmaids 9, 67–9, *67*, *68*, 78–80
Brunia albiflora 114, *156*
Brussels sprouts *121*, *123*
budgeting 11
buttonholes 69, *69*, 73, 74–7, *141*, 142

C

cabbages *56*, *109*, 111, 114, *116*, 121, *123*, 156
cakes 73, 109, *109*, 130–1, *142*
calla lilies *10*, 11, 38, *38*, *40*, *41*, 45, *45*, *47*, *51*, *57*, 70, *70–1*, 74, *92*, 92, *93*, 101, 119, *132*, 132, *133*, 146, 150, *151*, *152*, *154*, 157
Callistemon citrinus 155
Camellia 121, *141*, *142*
  x *williamsii* 'E.G. Waterhouse' *147*
candles 11–12, 108, 110, 114, 117
Capsicum annuum 150, *155*
carnations 67, 157
Carthamus tinctorius 'Kinko' *150*
cascade bouquets 44
celosia 20, 36, 74, 149, *152*, *153*
Centaurea montana *151*
centrepieces 108–9, 114–19, 134–5, *135*
ceremony flowers 86–103
Chaenomeles japonica 80, *147*
chairbacks 98–101, *101*, 108, *140*
Chamelaucium uncinatum *147*, 156
chillies 74
chrysanthemums 20, 124
  'Early Bird Red' *155*
  'Reagan Orange' *154*
  'Reagan Red' *155*
  'Reagan White' *20*, *157*
  'Salmon Fairie' *150*
  'Shamrock' *150*
  'Tom Pearce' *154*
chuppahs *90*, 91, *94*, 121
churches 89–91, *91*, 96–7
circlets 67–8, *71*
Cirsium japonicum 'Pink Beauty' *149*, *152*
civil ceremonies 91, 94
colour 45–6, 50, 89
conditioning flowers 15, 46
conserving bouquets 47
Consolida ajacis *148*, 149
cornflowers *19*, *31*, 124
corsages 69, *69*, *75*, *81*
cosmos 20, *21*, 32, *32*, *51*, 59
Cotinus coggygria 'Royal Purple' 74, *151*
cotoneaster berries *126*
cranberries *126*
Crataegus laevigata 'Paul's Scarlet' *149*
cream flowers 108
Crocosmia *108*, 150

D

Dahlia 74, *108*, 124, 149
  'Canberra' *153*
  'Karma Serena' *156*
  'Karma Thalia' *156*
daisies *19*, 124, *130*
date palm leaves 38, *39*, *41*, 98, 118
Delphinium 23, *24*, *95*, *106*
  Belladonna Group 'Blue Shadow' *151*
  Belladonna Group 'Sky Lady' *148*
  Belladonna Group 'Völkerfrieden' *148*
  'Faust' *151*
  'Lilac Arrow' *151*
  'Skyline' *148*, *151*
Dendrobium *154*, 157

Dianthus 149, *153*, 157
dill 35, *150*
dog collars 84, *84–5*

E

Easter lilies 114, 156, 157
equisetum *134–5*
eryngium 28, 34, 75
Eucalyptus 21, 34, 56, 138
  'Baby Blue' *140*
  ficifolia *147*
  pulverulenta *154*
Eucharis 77, 80
  amazonica 156, *157*
Euonymus fortunei 'Emerald 'n' Gold' 146
Euphorbia fulgens 21, 37, 121
  'Beatrix' *154*
  'Largo White' *156*
  'Quicksilver' *146*
Eustoma grandiflorum (lisianthus) *19*, *53*, *55*, 73, 110, *141*, 157
  'Alice White' *157*
  'Echo Pure White' *53*
  'Mariachi Pink' *149*
  'Moon Pink' *147*
  'Piccolo Yellow' *146*

F

Fagus sylvatica *154*
fatsia leaves 99
flax leaves 38, *39*, *41*, 77, *92*, 98, 118
florists 13–14, 107
flower balls 68
Forsythia 18, *146*
Freesia *148*, 157
fritillary, snake's-head 18
fruit 11–12, 38, *108*, *127*, 136, *136–7*

G

galax leaves *102–3*
gardenias 45, 48, 69, *78*, *136–7*
garlands 91
Genista *146*, 156
Gentiana 'Sky' *151*
Gerbera 74, 97
  'Chateau' *126*
  'Dark Serena' *149*
  germini *115*, *146*, *147*, *152*, 155
  jamesonii 'Bianca' *157*
  'Pinky Eye' *49*
Gladiolus 20
  'Addi' *155*
  'Esta Bonita' *154*
  'Mont Blanc' *156*
  'Priscilla' *147*
gloriosa lilies 128, *136–7*
Gossypium herbaceum *156*
grape hyacinths see *Muscari*
guelder rose 92
Gypsophila 44
  'Little White' *157*
  'Lucky Stars' *156*
  'Million Stars' *153*

H

hair, flowers in 66, *66*, 69, 80
hats 66, 69
headdresses 66, *67*, *68*, *71*, 79
heart wreaths 102, *102–3*
hebe 36, *37*
Helenium 'Moerheim Beauty' *150*
Helianthus annuus 'Sonja' *150*
heliconia 97
hellebores 18, 80, *146*
herbs 32, *34*, 35, 44, *107*
Hippeastrum (amaryllis) 21, 36, 92, *121*, *122*, *123*, 155, 156
  'Ludwig Dazzler' *156*
  'Mont Blanc' *122*
  'Red Lion' *155*
  'Rilona' *154*
hoops 80
hops 26, *26*, 32
hosta leaves *10*, 19, 22, *24*, 52
huckleberry foliage *136–7*
Hyacinthus orientalis *147*, *148*, 156
Hydrangea 20, 26, *27*, *31*, 80, 84, *89*, *107*, 110, *113*, 130
  arborescens 'Annabelle' *156*
  macrophylla 56, *150*, *151*
Hypericum 20, 74, 150, 157

I

ilex (holly) berries 21, *154*, 155
Iris 'Purple Rain' *148*
ivy 28, *31*, 34, *75*, 111, 115, *120*, *125*, 130

J

jasmine 9, *92*, *94*, 121
Jewish weddings *90*, 91, 94, 120–3, *121*

K

Kentia palm 38, *39*, 97

L

lavender *19*, 32
Leucadendron 'Safari Sunset' *155*
Leucanthemum vulgare 74
Leucocoryne 'Caravelle' *130*
Leucospermum
  cordifolium 'Tango' *154*
  reflexum 'Lutea' *150*
Liatris spicata 'Blue Bird' *148*
lighting, receptions 108
ligustrum 77, *143*
lilac see *Syringa vulgaris*
Lilium (lilies) 20, 23, *96*
  'Casa Blanca' *26*, 156
  longiflorum 'Snow Queen' *157*
  longiflorum 'White Europe' *156*
  'Red Sox' *149*
  'Sissi' *24*
  'Star Gazer' 9
  see also arum lilies; calla lilies
lily-of-the-valley *8*, 9, *9*, 15, 45, 58, *92*, *93*, 109
lisianthus see *Eustoma grandiflorum*

love-in-a-mist *130*
love-lies-bleeding *20*
Lysimachia *130*, *141*, *142*
    clethroides *146*
    clethroides 'Helene' *153*

M
Malus x *robusta* 'Red Sentinel' *150*
marguerite daisies *124*, *130*
marjoram *8*
Matthiola incana *148*
millet grass *101*
Mimosa 'Yellow Island' *146*
mint *35*
mock orange see *Philadelphus*
Molucella laevis (bells of Ireland) *20*, *97*, *149*
monstera *38*, *39*, *121*
montbretia berries *74*
Muscari (grape hyacinths) *18*, *62–3*, *148*
    armeniacum 'Blue Dream' *148*
Myosotis sylvatica *148*

N
napkins *109*, *124–5*, *127–9*
Narcissus
    'Cheerfulness' *146*
    'Golden Ducat' *146*
    tazetta 'Ziva' *156*
necklaces *67*
nerines *20*, *21*

O
orange baskets *136*, *136–7*
orange blossom *8*, *66*
orange flowers *150*, *154*
orchids
    cymbidium *11*, *21*, *36*, *38*, *39*, *40*, *45*, *77*, *92*, *97*, *102–3*, *115*, *118*, *121*, *122*, *123*, *127*, *157*
    phalaenopsis *11*, *14*, *37*, *45*, *46*, *48*, *51*, *77*, *92*, *93*, *110*, *111*, *121*, *123*, *132*, *133*, *156*
        Singapore *11*, *36*, *45*, *69*, *80*
        slipper *19*, *40*
        vanda *81*, *98*
Ornithogalum thyrsoides 'Mount Fuji' *157*
outdoor weddings *89*
over-arm bouquets *48*, *51*, *57*

P
Paeonia (peonies) *10*, *18*, *22*, *22*, *24*, *51*, *80*, *106*
    'Bowl of Beauty' *147*
    'Duchesse de Nemours' *52*
    lactiflora 'Karl Rosenfield' *49*, *149*
    'Sarah Bernhardt' *53*, *147*
    'Shirley Temple' *49*
page boys *67*, *68*
Panicum miliaceum *152*
papyrus *38*, *39*, *92*, *111*, *121*
peonies see *Paeonia*
petals *68*, *89*, *91*, *109*, *143*

pew ends *90*, *97*, *101*
Philadelphus (mock orange) *8*, *106*
    'Virginal' *53*
Phlox 'Bright Eyes' *147*
Photinia x *fraseri* 'Red Robin' *155*
Physalis alkekengi *150*
pink flowers *45–6*, *147*, *149*, *152*
Pittosporum crassifolium
    'Variegatum' *146*
planning *14–15*
pomanders *68*, *82–3*, *83*
poppies, Icelandic *136–7*
Populus deltoides *146*, *150*
posies *9*, *9*, *48*, *52*, *60–3*, *69*
prayer books *68*, *80*
Protea *21*
    nerifolia *149*
Prunus *121*
    glandulosa 'Albo Plena' *146*
    serrulata *147*
purple flowers *148*, *151*
pussy willow *121*, *123*

Q
Quercus
    palustris *154*
    robur *154*

R
Ranunculus *18*, *74*, *106*, *129*, *130*
    'Pauline Burgundy' *136–7*
    'Pauline Scarlet' *155*
    'Ranobelle Donkergeel' *146*
    'Ranobelle Inra' *147*, *154*, *156*
reception flowers *88*, *104–43*
red flowers *155*
ribbons, bouquets *46–7*
ring-bearers *68*

Rosa (roses) *8*, *28*, *110*, *113*, *134–5*
    pomanders *82–3*, *83*
    rose dome bouquet *60–1*, *61*
    rose petals *68*, *89*, *91*, *109*, *143*
    rosehips *56*, *74*, *108*
    'Akito' *45*, *45*, *75*, *92*, *157*
    'Aqua' *147*, *152*
    'Aretha' *53*
    'Avalanche' *10*, *28*, *69*, *156*
    'Barbie' *75*, *130*
    'Bianca' *75*, *120*, *153*
    'Bianca Candy' *19*, *69*, *138*, *140–3*
    Black Baccara *21*, *34*, *55*, *70*, *75*, *102–3*, *131*, *155*
    'Blue Curiosa' *10*, *28*, *29*
    'Blue Gene' *10*, *28*, *110*, *151*
    'Blue Moon' *44*, *151*
    canina *155*
    'Cool Water' *75*
    'Deep Secret' *44*
    'Dolce Vita' *130*
    'Duo Unique' *152*
    'Emerald' *75*
    'Extase' *149*
    'Golden Gate' *150*

'Grand Prix' *11*, *36*, *45*, *49*, *56*, *75*, *84*, *97*, *108*, *115*, *126*, *155*
    'Iceberg' *114*, *132*, *157*
    'Illusion' *152*
    'Jacaranda' *74*, *149*, *152*
    'Laminuette' *70*, *147*
    'Liberty' *36*
    'Macarena' *154*
    'Milano' *55*, *75*, *111*, *131*, *136–7*, *147*, *149*
    'Milva' *75*, *108*
    'Mimi Eden' *152*
    'Narangar' *131*
    'Queensday' *136–7*
    'Rosita Vendela' *130*
    'Ruby Red' *131*
    'Saint Celia' *149*
    'Scented Pink' *140*
    'Sterling Silver' *28*
    'Tamango' *67*, *79*
    'Tamora' *49*
    'Taxi' *75*, *146*
    'Tressor 2000' *131*
    'Vendela' *62–3*, *70*, *71*, *75*, *77*, *83*, *141*, *142*
    virginiana *153*
    'Xtreme' *34*, *125*
rosemary *8*, *22*, *25*, *32*, *34*, *35*, *77*, *107*, *110*, *111*, *113*, *157*
roses see *Rosa*
rudbeckia *74*
ruscus *73*

S
sage *34*, *35*
Sandersonia aurantiaca *150*
Scabiosa
    caucasica 'Clive Greaves' *151*
    caucasica 'Hermina' *153*
    stellata 'Ping Pong' *151*
scented flowers *8–9*, *107–8*
Scilla siberica *148*
Sedum telephium 'Mohrchen' *152*
seed heads *20*, *21*
Senecio *77*, *114*
shoes *67*, *68*, *79*
shower bouquets *44*, *48*, *48*
Skimmia *21*, *84*, *102–3*, *108*, *125*, *126*
    japonica 'Rubella' *155*
snake grass *39*, *41*, *92*, *93*, *122*, *124*
snowberries see *Symphoricarpos*
Solanum integrifolium *109*, *154*
Solomon's seal *19*, *92*, *146*
Sorbus aria 'Lutescens' *149*
Spiraea nipponica 'Snowmound' *146*
spring flowers *18–19*, *21*, *22–5*, *146–8*
Stachys byzantina *8*
stephanotis *8*, *22*, *22*, *30*, *48*, *54*, *66*, *67*, *68*, *92*, *93*, *121*, *142*, *157*
stocks *23*
summer flowers *19–20*, *26–31*, *149–51*
sunflowers *12–13*, *74*, *150*

sweet peas *8*, *9*, *15*, *22*, *22*, *23*, *31*, *44*, *45*, *47*, *62–3*, *67*, *72*, *73*, *80*, *92*, *106*, *130*, *138*, *142*, *146*, *147*, *148*, *149*, *151*, *153*
symbolism *8*
Symphoricarpos (snowberries) *19*, *69*, *140–2*
    albus 'White Pearl' *153*
    x *doorenbosii* 'Red Pearl' *140*
    x *doorenbosii* 'White Hedge' *152*
    'Pink Pearl' *152*
Syringa vulgaris (lilac) *121*, *156*
    'Andenken an Ludwig Spaeth' *148*
    x *hyacinthiflora* 'Esther Staley' *148*
    'Primrose' *156*

T
table centrepieces *106*, *108–9*, *114–19*, *134–5*, *135*
table linen *109*
table settings *124–9*
themes *12–13*, *108*
throwing bouquets *46*, *47*
thyme *34*
Trachelium caeruleum
    'Album' *153*
    'Blue Wonder' *148*
traditions *13*
tuberose *14*, *92*, *92*, *114*, *138*, *141*, *146*
tulips *11*, *18*, *124*
    'Black Parrot' *148*
    'Lucky Strike' *147*
    'Monte Carlo' *146*
    'Prinses Irene' *154*
    'Prominence' *155*
    'Salmon Parrot' *147*
    'Upstar' *147*
    'Weber's Parrot' *146*

V
vegetables *21*
Veronica *31*
    longifolia 'Blauriesen' *148*
Viburnum *19*, *20*
    opulus *9*, *10*, *22*, *22*, *23*, *28*, *45*, *47*, *51*, *55*, *61*, *106*, *121*, *136–7*, *146*, *149*
    tinus *74*
violets *18–19*

W
wheat *12*, *26*, *26*, *68*
white flowers *45*, *46*, *89*, *92*, *108*, *153*, *156*
winter flowers *21*, *36–41*, *155–6*
wiring flowers *44*
wreaths *102*, *102–3*, *107*
wrist corsages *67*, *69*, *78*

Y
yellow flowers *146*, *150*, *153*

Z
Zantedeschia aethiopica see arum lilies; calla lilies
zinnias *20*, *124*

acknowledgements

author Firstly this book would not have been possible without the wonderful brides and grooms who allowed us to share in their special day. Thanks to you all, past and present, over the last fifteen years and to the following brides whose weddings have been shown in this book: Claire Bailey, Shelly-Ann Bowdler, Natalie Chamberlain, Naomi Cuthbert, Anna Dalton-Knott, Monica Gillett, Julie Harper, Jane Houghton, Natalia Kudimova, Penny Mallinson, Sarah Miller, Annabel Pincus, Bella Pringle, Jenny Reid, Karen Sear, Keren Spier.

Thank you to all the featured venues: The Carlton Towers Hotel, London SW1; Claridges, London W1; Coq D'Argent, London EC2; Eltham Palace, Kent; Fredericks Restaurant, London N1; The Hempel Hotel, London W2; Le Manoir aux Quat' Saisons, Oxfordshire; Anton Mosimann and everyone at Mosimanns Club, London SW1; The Naval and Military Club, London SW1; The Orangery, London W11; Pallazo Pisani in Venice, Italy; The Royal Air Force Club, London W1; The Royal Geographic Society London SW7; The Savoy Hotel, London WC2; Six Hamilton Place, London W1; Syon House and Conservatory, London TW8

Thank you to all the party planners, wedding organisers, caterers and banqueting staff we have had the pleasure of working with over the years – in particular Lionel Benjamin and all at the Savoy; Joseph Cote and the team at Claridges; Peter Prescott at Conran Restaurants; and the Carlton Towers Hotel. Thank you to all the caterers we have worked with in this book; Jalpeno who organised the wedding at Syon House and Rochelle Sassoon who organised Keren and Dani Spier's wedding. Thanks also to Bluebird 2 You, London SW3; Tony Page, London NW10; Carole Sobell, London NW9; and Kate Pouler of Pat-A-Cake (020 7485 0006) and Mich Turner at the Little Venice Cake Company (020 7486 5252) for their help with the cake section. Thank you also to the wedding organisers including Sophie Lillingstone (020 7384 0684) for her help with Monica Gillett's wedding.

A huge thank you to Karen Pocock and all at the Wedding Shop both in the Fulham Road and at Liberty for all their assistance. Also to Vera Wang for creating the dresses that made so many of the brides featured in this book look perfect on their wedding day. A special thanks to the staff at the Wedding Shop at Liberty for the feature on pages 48–9 of the gorgeous Vera Wang dresses. Thank you also to Jacques Azagury; Christina Couture; Ritva Westinuo.

It was my great pleasure to work with Chris Tubbs, who so calmly and beautifully photographed many of our weddings and added his creativity to the still-life photographs. An enormous thank you to Valerie Fong, my art director, who kept us on track and gave her all to this project and has been responsible for making it into this stunningly beautiful book. Thank you also to Valerie for her good humour and patience throughout! Thanks to Emma Callery who started off as my editor, for her input, and an enormous thanks to Vicki Vrint who picked up the project halfway through and managed to get me to meet the deadline in the most professional and enduring manner! Thanks for all your hard work and for all the people behind the scenes who have worked on the production – in particular Geoff Barlow. Thank you to the Paula Pryke team who have been very supportive throughout the making of this book – in particular to Samantha Griffiths, Ashleigh Hopkins, Sarah Jackson, Julie Redden – and to all our wonderful suppliers, especially Dennis Edwards and all the hard-working growers. It has also been my pleasure to work with Pascal Plessis and all the photographers at Contre-Jour (see right) who provided photographs of weddings that we worked on together over the years.

Finally thanks to my bridegroom Peter for his love and support and for sixteen wonderful years together!

All photographs are by Chris Tubbs except for those taken by: Paula Pryke – p93 top & far right Contre-Jour, 40 Martell Road, London, SE21 4EN (020 8670 1234) – p13 all; p14 bottom right; p36-7 all; p45 top left; p46 all; p47 bottom; p51 top left; p70-73 all; p88; p91 top left & bottom; p92 all; p93 bottom left & bottom right; p99; p107 top right; p109 bottom